C. S. LEWIS

At Home in Ireland

About a Saint & Scholar

from the County Down :

C. S. LEWIS

At Home in Ireland

A CENTENARY BIOGRAPHY

with best wishes

for :

David Bleakley

DAVID BLEAKLEY

St Patrick's-tide, 2001 AD

FOREWARD BY WALTER HOOPER

STRANDTOWN PRESS
8 THORNHILL, BANGOR, CO. DOWN, BT19 1RD

C. S. LEWIS - at Home in Ireland
First published 1998

Copyright © 1998 D. W. Bleakley

ISBN 1 898787 67 0

Strandtown Press
8 Thornhill, Bangor,
BT19 1RD
Telephone Bangor: 454898

A C. S. Lewis Centenary Imprint

**Distributed by Eason, Ireland
(Belfast: T. 381200; Dublin: T. 8622111
www. eason. ie**

Printed by JC Print Ltd., Belfast

Dedication

To my grandchildren,
Iain and Mark, Stephanie and Gavin,
and to 'children' everywhere;

may they discover the magic which is C.S. Lewis.

The Searcher (by Ross Wilson)
C.S. Lewis Centenary Sculpture
Holywood Arches Library, Belfast,
6 November, 1998

Contents

Message from President McAleese

As President and as a Belfast woman, I pleased to be associated with the centenary commemoration of the birth of one of Belfast's great Christians and writers, C.S.Lewis, and the celebration of his life and work.

C.S. Lewis, though working and living at Oxford, never lost contact with his beloved Belfast and North County Down It is as though he reverted again and again to his happy childhood years to make sense of the world in which he lived and worked in later life. For those of us who were fortunate to have lived in both Belfast and Co. Down, it is easy to understand the draw that brought him back - and the happiness he found on his visits to that unique part of the world.

Yet it was his experiences outside his native Ireland, as much as his many years there, that were to have such an influence on him as a writer and as a Christian. In his conversion to Christianity at the significant age of 33, he was reconciled with God, and his message of reconciliation was to be an important element in his writings as a Christian. In these eventful days of new hope and optimism in Northern Ireland, it is both poignant and prophetic that we should be recalling the life and work of one of its sons, as we too work towards reconciliation between the traditions, cultures and creeds of communities that have been so torn by strife and bitterness.

Lewis was concerned with the message of Christ; a message without frontiers, simple and direct, it commanded us to love one another. That commandment challenges us to transcend denom-in-ationalism, to rise above difference, and to offer love to those whom we find it most difficult to love. The transforming effect of love on a world inured to hatred is the vision Christians profess to seek.

In celebrating C.S. Lewis in his centenary year, we look to him for inspiration in the coming months and years, drawing on his wisdom to show those who profess to be Christians how to generously open up our hearts and minds to the other Christians with whom we share this place and these days.

Mary McAleese
President

Foreword

BY WALTER HOOPER

C.S. Lewis always thought in terms of the particular: this man, this book, this cup of tea. He was, naturally, impatient with the vague and the general, and this is why his works are so clear and solid.

The same can be said of this delightful book. Of the millions of words written in celebration of the Centenary of Lewis' birth, David Bleakley's seem to me the most valuable. They lift the particular onto a high level, and by concentrating on Lewis and his native Ireland they illuminate an area of Lewis' life no-one has written about before. The glorious particulars of Strandtown – Dundela Villas, Little Lea, St.Marks Church, the Ewart family, Glenmachan House, Gelston's Corner, Horatio Todds Chemist Shop – all are forever inseparable from Lewis . More than that, for me the mention of them has solved a puzzle that has been on my mind many years. I once asked Lewis if he ever went to France. 'Don't you remember,' he said, 'I was there during the war.' 'But', I said, 'that was in 1918 when you were fighting on the Somme.' 'It was enough,' he replied, and he went on to talk about an approaching trip to Ireland. I see now that, while Lewis was happy to have the rest of the world mediated to him through books, County Down was home, and he could be there often enough.

But if I may be even more particular about the virtues I have found here, I doubt if any amount of 'Lewis scholarship' can provide us with as much truth as Mr. Bleakley's little anecdote about Heaven. He tells us that sometime after he became a student in Oxford, Lewis asked him to define Heaven. After some 'theological meanderings' on David's part, Lewis supplied the answer: ' Heaven is Oxford lifted and placed in the middle of the County Down.' That alone makes this book worth its weight in gold, for it sums up almost all that Lewis loved and that made him the particular man he was.

CHAPTER ONE

Quest for Lewis in Ireland —
a Prologue

During 1996 the following letter about C.S. Lewis appeared in newspapers throughout Britain and Ireland. It was a signal that Ireland had awakened to the duty and responsibility of celebrating the Centenary of one of its greatest sons. A particular need was felt to underline his Irish identity and to emphasise the importance of his formative years in Belfast and the County Down.

As the letter put it:

C.S.LEWIS
Sir,

   Christians in Ireland are preparing to celebrate the 1998 Centenary of C.S. Lewis' birth. A Centenary Committee has been formed in Belfast to promote the occasion and to gather information about Lewis in his local setting.

*As co-ordinator of the search for 'Lewis of Little Lea'
I am anxious to hear from any who knew him during his
work in England and who may be able to share with us
signs of his interest in his homeland - in particular, his
beloved County Down and the 'village' of Strandtown,
his birthplace. Any information would be gratefully
received as a donation to our local celebration.*

*From personal links with the Lewis/Greeves family
circle, student days at Oxford and for some years as Member of Parliament for the Strandtown district, I know how
much we owe to the man, though Ireland has been slow to
acclaim his greatness. In 1998 we are anxious to make
amends, during what promises to be an event bringing
together our whole community in shared pride for one of
Ireland's greatest sons.*

*Yours, etc
David Bleakley*

When I wrote the letter I was conscious that time was 'getting
on' and that Lewis' Centenary would soon be upon us. It seemed
that few in Ireland were aware of the date or that one of Ireland's
greatest literary sons was in danger of being neglected in the land of
his birth.

Happily the letter produced a positive response from followers
far and wide who knew of the fame of Lewis and who had been
influenced by his writings and personality. There was also a general
consensus that the time had come to register the fact that C.S. Lewis
was very much an Irishman, proud of the land of his birth and deeply
influenced by the people and places of his homeland.

Since then much has been added to our knowledge of Lewis in
his Irish setting, augmenting the information base built up by those

who down the years have sought to maintain interest in our teacher and friend. Sometimes the information seems slight but, as Archbishop Donald Caird of Dublin reminds us in his letter, every 'pebble' helps to make a decent 'cairn'.

This 'biography' does not dwell on the literature of C.S.L. - the basic aim has been to concentrate on the places and people making him the boy he was and the man he ultimately became. But there is often parity of esteem between places and people. For this reason the Genesis story is very much a local account of things Lewis - based on 'round the fire' talk, indulged in by the Strandtown villagers, people whom he knew, who knew him and whose wisdom and native wit he often pondered upon. Some of his near contemporaries are still around and are able to provide verbal or written accounts of the time. Those of us from a younger generation have a memory bank based on the table talk of our parents. I think of my aunts and uncles who were part of the 'downstairs' domestic force, and of the many local artisans who served the specialist needs of the 'Big Houses'. Hopefully this Irish contribution will add to the fuller appreciation of Lewis' back-ground and the influence it exerted upon him.

In contacts with Lewis Societies outside Ireland I have been encouraged to believe so. Oxford and American contacts have been particularly helpful and encouraging: Michael Ward with his work at the Kilns; Mary Rogers with intimate knowledge of early days in Belfast; and especially Walter Hooper, who having an American's 'cousin-relationship' with Ireland, is well placed to understand the complexity which lies at the heart of Anglo-Irish relationships, even in the field of literature.

The ways into Lewis in his Irish setting are many, but the approach of this biography is that of a Strandtown man, born close to the Lewis homes and sharing in many of the social institutions around which the village and its County Down hinterland revolved.

The first and most helpful introduction to the search area is to belong to the circle of local inhabitants who made up the network which Lewis regarded with affection and regard. Not that many of Strandtown would have false delusions of grandeur except that we would recognise the social reality of the human network to which Lewis belonged and with which he shared a marked sense of belonging.

My own family roots are fairly typical, with a strong commitment to church and community service. So, though a humble student when Lewis was a famous Professor, we shared a knowledge and often common experience of the Strandtown neighbourhood. When discussing the district we knew the local 'shorthand' and recognised the social landscape. Surprisingly much of that landscape is still extant: some of the 'Big Houses' frequented by the Lewis boys can still be seen; the Ewart and Greeves and other founding families remain; and St. Mark's along with Belmont Presbyterian Church continues to serve. My personal overlap with C.S. Lewis, including a vital Oxford experience, was strengthened by a shipyard apprenticeship and shared Anglican links.

More coincidentally, during my period of public service as Member of Parliament for the Strandtown Constituency all three Lewis - connected houses, and 'Bernagh' as well, were within my political bailiwick. Even more happen-chance (such is village intimacy) the constituency was once in the possession of Captain O.W.J. (Bill) Henderson, son-in-law of Gundreda Forrest (née Ewart). Though of different political vintages we are the best of friends. And now that neither of us remains in Parliament we can join forces in assuring all-comers that there is, indeed, 'life after politics'! The Hendersons maintain the tradition of Ewart support for St. Mark's and have contributed much time and talent to the Centenary Celebration.

My wife, too, has been very much part of the Strandtown social network and has encouraged many family friends to join the 'Quest for Lewis'. By such means local human resources are harnessed and new Lewisians are recruited. So, in the company of like-minded good companions, it was natural that we should 'do something about 1998'. We have sought to make the response a shared occasion - a time to lay down markers about things Irish, and particularly things local, which may be of use to our own and future generations. We know, of course, that there is much more to Lewis than the Strandtown-Irish experience; and we know, too, that the wider Lewis family will not neglect its specialist agenda.

We trust that this Irish Biography will provide useful new pointers.

CHAPTER TWO

C.S. Lewis – *an Irish Homecoming*

T he Irish are a fair people; they never speak well of
one another.' That was Samuel Johnson writing to Dr.
Barnard, Bishop of Killaloe in 1775.

I do not recall C.S. Lewis ever complaining on this score, though
for much of his life he was never fully acknowledged by the Irish
community as 'one of their own'. Sometimes, indeed there were
those in literary circles who sought to serve an exclusion order on a
fellow countryman who did not conform to their all-too-narrow
definition of Irishness.

But more often than not it was simply a case of Lewis being 'out
of sight, out of mind'; he did not behave as a stage Irishman nor
were his erudite early works likely to make him a best-seller in the
Irish popular market.

This non-recognition of Lewis' Irishness has been aided and
abetted in works of literary reference which insist on an English
birth certificate. For example, the Oxford Dictionary of Quotations
has given the misleading listing of 'C.S. Lewis 1898 - 1963, English

Literary scholar.' For Louis MacNiece, a close contemporary, they tried harder: 'British poet born in Belfast.'

More surprisingly, the massive Dictionary of Irish Literature, revised and expanded in 1996 (Aldwych Press, London) manages to engage in a detailed survey of Irish writers without marking Lewis out for special mention. The compilers trawl far and wide (they even, and rightly, give credit to popular Irish comedian Spike Milligan, for his interesting autobiography). But C.S. Lewis gets no real examination; all he receives is a tiny footnote on two occasions, and then only in reference to the work of others.

Robert Hogan, Editor in Chief of the Dictionary, makes a point in his excellent preface; 'Not every Irish author...has been thought important enough to be accorded a separate listing in the body of the new work.' Hopefully C.S. Lewis will have 'made the grade' when a new Edition of the Irish Dictionary is published.

However, not all English-based literary guides offend. For example, the Oxford Companion to Irish Literature, 1996, offers a scholarly comment by Dr. John Gillespie, a Coleraine university don, who along with Professor Robert Walsh of the University of Ulster, has done much to raise the profile of Lewis in Ireland and further afield. In addition, 'The Oxford Book of Ireland' (a magnificent compilation of things Irish) in its 1998 collection of some of 'the best writers in the world brought together to celebrate the nation and its people', makes mention of Lewis on two occasions - both quotations from **Surprised by Joy.**

Perhaps the delay in giving Lewis the all-island recognition he deserved has had something to do with the universality of an appeal which made it difficult for him to be fitted into conventional Irish categories. Billy Graham's observation that Lewis was essentially 'an unassuming and humble spiritual giant' provides another possible clue to the neglect.

More analytical is Conor Cruise O'Brien's penetrating observation (Ancestral Voices, 1994) about what he calls the 'recklessly idiosyncratic' definitions of what is 'Irish-Ireland' which were beginning to emerge around 1900 and which for a time caused furious debate within Irish society. As O'Brien described the 'new look' Nationalist: 'He or she is Catholic, preferably, but if not Catholic, then thoroughly deferential to Catholic-nationalists, on all questions relating to the definitions and practices of Irish-Ireland ... He or she is passionately opposed to all forms of English influence in Ireland, including the playing of foreign games, such as cricket and rugby, and therefore supports the Gaelic Athletic Association.'

Lewis, who was born around this time (and in the Province of Ulster), did not fit in with this view of things nor would he have wanted to; he and many others felt marginalised and through no fault of their own became literary symbols of a wider national debate.

So in the deeply divided Ireland which emerged after 1921, 'which side are you on!' became a question not easy to answer for the many who did not feel part of what became a cultural as well as a political divide. Local writers like Forrest Reid, John Hewitt, St. John Ervine, Sam Hanna Bell and Sam Thompson felt the strain. Those who lived outside the island still felt pressure, but it was different in range and intensity.

Scholars like C.S. Lewis whose cultural workbench was in Oxford were able to get on with their work (often in Studies far removed from Irish politics) without having to relate to the cultural mores of their native land. But they could not escape the reckoning when a listing of the 'truly Irish' was being compiled by those on the spot.

Seamus Heaney, Ireland's great poet and Nobel Prize Winner for Literature, who has done so much to give Ireland a sense of cultural oneness and a renewed world literary status, was an acute observer of the literary scene in the 1950s at Queen's University. His views on an 'unlocalised' Lewis reflect much of the feeling of the time and yet presage the transition that is currently taking place as pre-Centenary reassessments have been set in train. In later years Seamus, while Professor of Poetry at Oxford, had an opportunity to learn more about his fellow Ulsterman in a wider intellectual setting as one of 'the age of the giants'. Generously, this Poet of the People, shares his memories of C.S.L . and encourages our Centenary initiative : -

FROM: SEAMUS HEANEY, DUBLIN 4.

As an undergraduate at Queen's University in the 1950s, I read C.S. Lewis' epoch making work, The Allegory of Love, and his volume in The Cambridge History of English Literature dealing with the prose and poetry of the sixteenth century. By then his name was enshrined, his voice authoritative, scholarly, unlocalized. It never occurred to us that be might have a biography, never mind come from Belfast. Had we known that, his writings might have taken a more personal hold upon our understanding.

Later on I was elected a Fellow of Magdalen College during my tenure of the Professorship of Poetry at Oxford. There too I was conscious of Lewis' presence, not so much as a predecessor from Ireland, more as a naturalized citizen of Oxbridge, a "character", one of the names that evoked the academic equivalent of the age of the giants - the Oxford of Tolkien and Sparrow and Starkie and Bowra.

In this Centenary year, therefore, it is good to be reminded of Lewis' Ulster birth and connections, and to

ask whether there might be any connection between his
first place and his final achievement, whether and how
the combination of his Irish background and his English
arrival might have affected his scholarly ambitions, his
writerly vocation and his religious bent.

5 April, 1998

A formidable comment and agenda from Seamus Heaney and worthy of the homecoming celebration of C.S. Lewis as we prepare for his Centenary year. The signs are good and the timing is historic. Over many decades a new and liberating consensus has been developing in Ireland, helping us to reach out to one another and to the wider world which our forebears have explored. So much so that a sea-change in public opinion has taken place. It is based on a parity of esteem between our contending traditions; and it represents a spiritual pluralism in which minds like C.S. Lewis are free-to-be.

This letter from Seamus Heaney is one of many brought together in this Irish companion to illustrate our theme. The correspondents range far and wide and convey the many-sidedness of their subject. For many years they have been fellow seekers for the pollen of peace in Ireland's fields of conflict.

Lewis would have liked their comments, and would have pondered their arguments. But, I suspect, that he would have warmed especially to the letters from the children of Mersey Street Primary School (the 'shipyard' school) in the heart of his beloved East Belfast and near to 'Ty-Isa', the home of his grandfather, Richard, and a favourite stopover for Jack and Warnie.

Other Irish artists have signalled their intention of marking C.S. Lewis' Centenary. A special contribution, and of a permanent nature, comes from Ross Wilson, one of Ireland's most exciting sculptors. His tribute takes the form of a life-size bronze statue which is to be placed at Holywood Arches in East Belfast, an area well-known to the Lewis family. The study which has been created by Ross Wilson is entitled 'Searching for Narnia' and the figure and wardrobe will be life-size. Ross, like many from 'Young Ireland', is keenly aware of Lewis' spiritual and national significance. He describes his bronze sculpture thus: 'The image of the man walking towards the wardrobe is a stylized heroic image of C.S. Lewis, representing the searcher: an almost everyman, setting out to find Narnia and Aslan.'

Our sculptor's description is thought provoking: 'I hope it will be a pointer as well, to show that sometimes the greatest things can be found in the unlikelyist of places, a wardrobe, a world beyond a wardrobe.'

In the completed model the sculptor has replaced the book with a chair: 'The finished figure will hold a chair and not a book. The chair may, and I hope will, be used as a means of transport: as the viewer (children viewers to the fore) is seated on the bronze chair they travel through Lewis via imagination to Narnia. A way of helping people review things, like their very next thoughts.'

In a borrowing on Lewis, the sculptor reminds us that we are all statues in a worldly sculptor's shop and that eventually, some of us are going to come to life! I like to think that Ross Wilson's creation will animate those who view it.

The Holywood Arches (called after a local railway crossing) site is well chosen. It is the famous Belfast meeting point of Strandtown and Ballymacarrett - formerly separate village communities It was an area much frequented by the Lewis brothers when they visited the home of their favourite grandfather Richard in nearby 'Ty-Isa' (Welsh for 'little house on its own'), still extant and in good condition. Today the 'Arches' remains a meeting point for the children of the area who, Lewis would be glad to know, are provided with a well stocked public library.

For those who wish to explore the special world of Strandtown and Belmont the Arches is an appropriate place from which to start. Lewis knew it well and it is a place evocative of happy childhood times spent in the neighbourhood by Warnie and brother Jack, inseparable then, as later in life. Incidentally, I usually use the description C.S. Lewis, C.S. or C.S.L. rather than 'Jack'. Indeed, apart from within the Lewis /Ewart/Greeves family circle in Ireland and the Oxford fraternity, I have found few locally who used the name which Lewis invented for himself while still a child. Class was a considerable factor in early 20th Century Belfast -'Master Jack' would be about as familiar as most locals would have ventured.

'Lewis of Little Lea' is another description used locally. But while Albert Lewis was alive it was <u>he</u> and not his son who was associated in the public mind with the new house in the neighbourhood of elegant Circular Road. In fact, in his day 'the house that Albert built' was quite a talking point among artisans like George Heatherington and others who cared for the fabric and fittings of the new dwelling on Circular Road. They could never quite understand why he denigrated the place which they regarded as 'a bit of a mansion' and 'up to date' by the standards of the day.

'Little Lea' is still very much a private family home and is well cared for by its owners, Denis and Margaret Rogers.

Interest in Lewis and his Irish roots was considerably stimulated by such local responses and by the 1990s it seemed timely to examine the family circumstances in greater detail. So local and national newspapers were told of the 'Irish Quest for Lewis' and of the need for public assistance in the search. Happily the initiative was widely interpreted as a signal that Ireland should awake to the opportunity to celebrate the life and work of its famous son. Since then it has been a case of patiently collecting the pebbles of information that remain on the Irish shore. The pieces have varied in rarity value but, brought together with longer accumulated personal records, they provide a 'way into' Lewis' Irish Genesis. It has been a worth-while and at times exciting search.

As a final stage in research I was encouraged to send a personal letter to a selection of people throughout Ireland, well placed to comment on the significance of Lewis to them and for our time.

Dear Friend,

C.S. Lewis Centenary, 1998

I write to ask a special favour. It is about C.S. Lewis , a mutual friend about whom we have sometimes talked. 1998 gives us a chance to mark his Centenary.

I write to ask if you would honour and encourage the occasion with a word of appreciation for C.S.L . and for his significance in Ireland today. I am anxious to put the 'pieces' together in time for the Commemoration

In your busy life it is much to ask, but I know that a word from you would do much to raise awareness for one of Ireland's greatest sons.

With best wishes and gratitude for all you do for our land.

Yours sincerely,

David Bleakley
8 Thornhill, Bangor, Co. Down.

The response to this personal approach was impressive. It came from men and women who had been influenced by Lewis, remembering him as a warm human being and as a revered teacher. Some were internationally famous and many were acknowledged leaders in their field. Lewis would have respected their comments though probably succumbing to the easy embarassment which Billy Graham has noted.

Lewis would also have been touched by the evidence which has been accumulated from those who knew him in his everyday Strandtown context. From, for instance, Strandtown: the local milkman, the breadserver, servants like Annie Strahan and May Jamison who were with him during difficult times, the traders who had served him across the counter, a man who 'kept the cars on the road and fixed the bicycles' - and others in the servant class who had known 'Master Jack' as a member of the ' Big Houses' with which he had family links and which they helped to run.

The human panorama provided by such witnesses is revealing. C.S. Lewis with his knowledge of 19th Century 'Big House' literature would have appreciated the views of family retainers. He never underestimated the symbiosis that existed between 'upstairs and downstairs' in the households of his day; nor did those who replied to my public appeal.

C.S.L. would have enjoyed in particular the delightfully personal word of thanks which James Galway sent. Writing from Switzerland this ebullient and ever popular 'Man with the Golden Flute' had this to say:

Meggan, Switzerland, 14 June, 1997

Dear David,

I had no idea C.S. Lewis was an Irishman and I am so proud to learn this. He is my very favourite writer and I *am currently struggling through **Mere Christianity** which is a truly wonderful opus. What a gifted man he is. He has given me a great deal to be thankful for.*

It is wonderful to hear that he is going to be honoured locally and universally in his Centenary year. I have always spoken of him with my Christian friends, but now I can do so with pride, knowing he is an Irishman and born only a stone's throw from where I was born.

Yours sincerely and best wishes for the project.

James Galway

James Galway catches the happy spirit which is C.S. Lewis.

In this Centenary Year that generous spirit is permeating the whole of Ireland. Island-wide, our people are joining in the homecoming for C.S. Lewis; he is being owned by all four Provinces. The gracious message which we have received from President Mary McAleese, herself from Belfast, symbolises the new consensus. In particular, President Mary underlines the relevance of C.S. Lewis to our time. As she puts it :

'Lewis was concerned with the message of Christ; a message without frontiers, simple and direct, it commanded us to love one another. That commandment challenges us to transcend denominationalism, to rise above differences, and to offer love to those whom we find it most difficult to love. The transforming effect of love on a world inured to hatred is the vision Christians profess to seek.

In celebrating C.S. Lewis in his Centenary Year, we look to him for inspiration in the coming months and years, drawing on his wisdom to show those who profess to be Christians how to generously open up our hearts and minds to the other Christians with whom we share this place these days.'

The President's sentiments are a happy rejoinder to Dr. Johnson's cynical quip which opened this Chapter.

CHAPTER THREE

Oxford and Cambridge –
Teacher and Friend

D irect Irish contacts with Lewis are becoming 'thin on the ground', but it is a tribute to the personality of the man that time has done little to diminish gratitude for the privilege of knowing him.

Many of my correspondents have written to me in considerable detail. In addition I have been able to talk to them as personal friends of long standing. My aim has been to produce a 'conversation' based on an overlap of written and spoken word.

I have made little reference to published sources, which are readily available. Basically, I have preferred to sift through the many new pieces of information about our subject, which are coming to hand. The search has been for clues to Lewis' Irish identity.

My first witness is Mary Morwood who, with her husband-to-be (Rev. P. H. Rogers, Headmaster, Portora Royal School, Enniskillen 1954 - 73) was an undergraduate reading English at Oxford in 1932. Together they attended Lewis' famous 'Prolegomena to Medieval Studies' series and found him to be 'a stunning lecturer'. Mary, now living in Oxford with her husband 'Val', is another example of the comprehensive nature of Irish social networking. We have shared Lewis interests, but we have also engaged in Ireland on joint ventures to do with SCM work in schools and university. Another link has been with Mary's sister Elizabeth and her husband John Boyle, eminent social historians. Elizabeth's lovely book on the Irish lace makers, The Irish Flowerers, was much-appreciated in local Lewisian circles in the 1950s. Lewis favoured such research into Irish country life.

Mary Rogers' contribution to C.S. Lewis studies has been considerable and continues. She and her circle of friends kept the name of Lewis alive in the early days of his Oxford career. In particular, the 'Drawing Room Circle', founded by her mother in 1926 as a literary discussion group did much to provide a platform for local writers in Belfast and district. Mary's Circle also provided a valuable link with Jane (Janie) McNeill who was ever protective of Lewis' reputation and for whom Lewis had a deep, if somewhat bemused, regard. The warmth of Lewis' regard was delightfully and movingly expressed in his obituary notice for the Campbell College Magazine when Janie died in March 1959:

'What I remember is something as boisterous, often as discomposing but always as fresh and tonic, as a high wind. Janie was the delight and terror of a little Strandtown and Belmont circle, now almost extinct. She was a born satirist. Every kind of sham and self-righteousness was her butt. She deflated the unco-gude with a single ironic phrase, then a moment's silence, then the great gust of her laughter. She laughed with her whole body. When I consider how all this was maintained through years of increasing loneliness, pain, disability, and

inevitable frustration I am inclined to say she had a soul
as brave and uncomplaining as any I ever knew.'

Janie would have appreciated such a tribute - qualities not unlike those of Joy Davidman. Janie had close ties with the Drawing Room Circle, a group which, Mary Rogers believed, did much to inspire the eulogy of Strandtown and Belmont people in Surprised by Joy.

But Mary Rogers rightly stresses the wider dimension of Lewis' Irish attachment, which at times was in conflict with the Ewart/Lewis family view of things. As Mary put it to me:

> *'While I agree that he loved Strandtown, Belmont, the*
> *Holywood Hills and Crawfordsburn, I do not think he was*
> *solely a North of Ireland man. His father's and uncles'*
> *perpetual talk of Unionist politics made him intolerant of*
> *all politics. He felt as much at home in Donegal*
> *(Rathmullan) and Louth (Annagassan) as he did in*
> *Belfast. My own experience confirms this.*
>
> *And for the contemporary Irish, Mary points to Lewis*
> *as a man ahead of his time: - 'He was certainly a believer*
> *in the two traditions, making for richness, if allowed to*
> *do so, rather than conflict. Would that the lesson could be*
> *learnt! I hope that the Centenary of his birth will empha-*
> *sise that aspect of his life. He loved Celtic mythology,*
> *which is the heritage of all Irish people and he would*
> *have hated the violence and polarization of our times'.*

Mary also rebuts the suggestion that C.S.L. was a bit of a male chauvinist. She acknowledges that 'superficially Lewis seemed to exclude women from much of his life as a don and lecturer in the

1930s and 1940s. There were, for instance, no women present when the Inklings met in Lewis' room in Magdalen for tea or beer and to exchange 'brilliant, sometimes bawdy, literary badinage, as well as to share a reading of their latest writings with one another.' But, nevertheless, men and women students were treated alike: 'True scholars, clever and hardworking pupils had nothing to fear from him. He went to endless trouble to further their careers, both while they were up at Oxford, and after they had gone down.' I know through my own contacts with Ruskin College that this was so - he was ever ready to help as Lionel Elvin, our Principal, confirms (see letter).

Mary Rogers also pays tribute to the generosity of C.S. Lewis, particularly when he became a best seller. He set up an Agape Trust in order to share his sudden fortune and many neglected good causes were underwritten. Mary observes that this generosity got little thanks from those who resented his popular appeal. As she puts it: 'The Establishment, even if it had known that Lewis gave away what he earned through writing would still not have forgiven him, but just thought him idiotic, as usual.' However, as she concludes: 'Jack never minded looking a fool in a good cause.'

Mary Rogers has written up much of these views in a delightful essay, 'C.S. Lewis - God's Fool'.

Another woman student who has vivid memories of Lewis is Mollie Reidy of Malahide, Co. Dublin - she comes from a well known Roman Catholic family and was a student, 1929-32.

Mollie Reidy was a pioneer member of the society of Home Students which later became St. Anne's College and was in her day an enthusiastic member of the Catholic Evidence Guild. She was also a lifelong friend of fellow Roman Catholic Elaine Griffiths who, after graduating gained fame as a Tutor in English and Fellow of St. Anne's. Elaine Griffiths also owes much to Lewis and more particularly to her supervisor J. R. R. Tolkien whom she admired as a scholar rather than as a writer of fairy tales. However, it is generally accepted that it was through her contacts with Allen & Unwin that Tolkien's The Hobbit came to be published.

Mollie Reidy, born 1910, retains her Oxford enthusiasms and still does much to 'drum up' news of Lewis in the Dublin region. She is modest about her considerable achievements in a lifetime as an educationist and remains somewhat in awe of her favourite tutor. She is also generous with her time and information.

When I last talked to Mollie in her book-lined home in Malahide she promised to expand on our discussion. Here is what she had to say about C.S. Lewis as an outstanding teacher and a great human being:

C.S. LEWIS : from memory - by Mollie Reidy,
Oxford School of English 1929/32

As an undergraduate I was fortunate to be in Oxford at a time when one could hear many good lectures in the School of English. Of all I heard the most out-standing were from C.S. Lewis . He stood out at the time and he stands out still in my memory as a great and admirable teacher in the somewhat restricted form of university lectures to large mixed audiences. He was at the outset of his career; he made his mark quickly and effectively.

If you were studying English in the thirties of this century you could not avoid getting to know a little about this unusual but immensely real person. To me, he seems to have acquired through his home life and perhaps through his odd early education much of the quality of wholeness, which we admire and try to achieve these days.

Maybe some of us thought we could plunge straight away into medieval poetry without a term of introductory lectures, but how glad we were when we found ourselves listening to 'Prolegomena to Medieval Poetry'. Given a large lecture room to begin with, Lewis had the unusual experience of being moved with his increasing audience to an even larger room. It is difficult to analyse his success as a lecturer, but it was easy to enjoy his wide and deep learning, his ability to express himself clearly in words well-chosen and well-used made it easy to be grateful for the chance to listen to him making his own loved subject refreshingly interesting to many unexpecting students.

Did you ever feel your eyelids struggling to resist closure while your pen went on trying shakily to record what you thought you had just heard? This could happen and often did, to me at the final moments of a twelve o'clock lecture - but not with C.S. Lewis lecturing. He had a quality of 'aliveness' that seemed to communicate itself through his words to other minds. That quality was akin to his ever-growing wholeness; and yet he was already elderly when he experienced, through the entry of a new person into his life, what he tried to express in **A Grief Observed.**

As one who met Lewis only as a lecturer and that at the outset of his career, I should hesitate to try to follow his personal development from the agnostic youth who arrived at Oxford after his extraordinary experience of schools in England up to the point when he admitted having become, even though unwillingly, a Christian. As such, he seemed not to need the support available from membership of any particular denomination. Perhaps one could say that it took him a long time to discover in himself the reality of Christianity - something that had not been, as he thought, quite extinguished by his unhelpful early education. This is described in the wonderful account of his early life in Surprised by Joy.

Having in my student days not even contemplated trying to make any personal contact with so important an academic, I contrived in 1952 to approach him with queries about a short poem he had published in an English Catholic Journal. To me this poem expressed a suggestion of the need, in our days, to belong to a Church. In response to my letter I received a courteous reply from him explaining his position, which obviously satisfied him at the time. I was more than pleased that he answered personally a question it was hardly my business to ask.

One has numbers of friends, derived sometimes from periods in one's life or particular areas of experience. C.S. Lewis was the kind of man who could be a friend to anyone, be it his brother with whom he shared a rare intimacy; his father, whom he continued constantly to visit in Belfast when his life and work were in England; his wife, who helped introduce him to new realms of living; his thousands of mind-widened students; or those millions of readers delighted and enlarged, spiritually and mentally, by his writings.

(signed) Mollie Reidy, Malahide, Co. Dublin.
March 1997

Mollie Reidy continues to help in the quest for C.S. Lewis . She ranges near and far in search of supporters. Recently she told me that she had telephoned Chicago and had a conversation with her

100 year-old friend, Sister Cyrille Gill, O.P., whom she first met at Oxford in 1930. Mollie's latest message to me is about the Sister: -

'She was in good form and delighted to be called - but I haven't yet got her to write any of her memories of C.S. Lewis.'

Knowing Mollie, she will keep on trying!

Mollie Reidy is, indeed, a worthy follower of C.S. Lewis and a splendid example of a grateful student following in his footsteps. Out of a fund of memories of her beloved teacher she has a favourite which I often quote. She once asked Lewis to expand on his story about foolish 'lost' people who blamed their 'map' for leading them astray. Molly has never forgotten his response. It went something like this: 'We have to remember that when we do not find in ourselves the fruits of the spirit which all our teachers promised, it is not that the promise was false, but that we have failed to use the grace we have been given. The map (C.S. Lewis reminded Molly) can be found in any Christian teaching.'

Mollie Reidy's vivid descriptions of her former tutor are not unusual - all whom I have approached have been ready to share their memories. Even a casual inquiry will evoke interest. Recently at a Church committee meeting in Edinburgh I made a passing remark about my Lewis research project. Nansie Blackie, a noted educationist in Scotland and a well-known local writer with close Irish links, was one of our group and noted my search for information. Her interest was immediate - by post came a quick response, short, but packed with penetrating observations:

**A MEMORY OF C.S. LEWIS: by Nansie Blackie,
April 1998**

Apart from my individual tutors - and more than many of those – no-one from my years at Oxford remains in my memory so clearly as C.S. Lewis in his capacity as host and chair of the Socratic Club which met on Saturday evenings. I went up to Oxford with the intention of reading Philosophy, Politics and Economics, and my primary interest was modern philosophy and its relation to theology, so Lewis' cast of mind was immediately sympathetic. His great gift was in the encouragement of open and honest discussion over wide areas of enquiry into truth. Given his expansive personality, he was curiously not intimidating. I realise now that this was largely due to his warmth and humour, the product of his Irish background. Those crowded and argumentative meetings had a vitality and informality in welcome contrast - for a Scot - to a somewhat chillier 'English' ambience of much Oxford life. 'The Screwtape Letters' delighted us and over the years I have never met a more effective communicator of Christian apologetic.

Nansie Blackie (Anderson) L.M.H. 1941-3, 1945-7.

I appreciated this tribute from a friend of long standing, who was a fellow student at Oxford during the 1940s. Together we were part of many an enthusiastic C.S.L. occasion.

My final witness from those who shared C.S. Lewis' academic life comes from Bishop Simon-Barrington Ward, who is of County Down stock and well versed in Irish affairs. He and I served together with the Church Mission Society - he as General Secretary and I as President. On many occasions during our mission travels we had an opportunity to discuss our favourite Christian apologist. I learnt much about Lewis' academic life from my General Secretary and friend.

Simon, himself a considerable writer and scholar, appreciates the impact which C.S.L. made on a post-war generation which after 1945 was seeking new spiritual guidelines. He points out:

> *'C.S. Lewis had an enormous influence on many members of my generation, a generation which came to maturity in the aftermath of the Second World War and in its search for an adequate response to some of the tragic events of our century found new spiritual roots and fresh springs in the Christian gospel as expressed by Lewis in a way which spoke to our heads, our hearts and our imagination. Ultimately it was his sure moral perception and his astonishing gift for parable and allegory, his capacity for presenting what he so felicitously called 'mere Christianity' in a way which transcended every denominational or sectarian boundary which made his message essentially one of reconciliation. In all these ways the freshness and scope of his witness have a message for all of us and perhaps especially for his own country of Ireland as it faces a cross-roads in its history.'*

Years later in 1956 at an important and difficult phase in Lewis' life he and Simon Barrington-Ward met up in Cambridge where Simon was Chaplain at Magdalene and C.S.L. a Professor. The effect of Lewis on his new College and University was profound. For Simon Barrington-Ward it was a particularly revealing and unforgettable personal experience. Simon shared this impression with me: - 'I first came to Magdalene College, Cambridge in 1956 as Chaplain, I looked forward to someone sympathetic and sensitive with whom I felt, in one's usual egotistical fashion, that I would be able to talk about myself and my faith and clarify many things. I imagined that he also would express similar confidences. But the person I actually met was a bluff red-faced farmer given to kindly and genial exchanges of a very general nature, keeping personal matters at arms length but enjoying the general, the metaphysical and literary, even the whimsically fantastic. I never seemed to get any nearer to him and indeed, after innumerable walks together and agreeable evenings, in which he was so often very kind to any visitor whom I brought in or to undergraduates whom I invited him to meet, I could have felt even further away than when I first began. Yet strangely enough, in some uncanny way, I suddenly began to realise that I really knew him quite well and quite intimately. One evening he invited me up to his room after dinner, a rare treat, and we talked about my work and his and be showed me some books and gave me what still remains a treasured copy of **The Allegory of Love**. Suddenly I realised that all this while as I seemed to be no nearer but even further away, I had actually been reaching the very point of deeper friendship which I had despaired of. It was a typical Lewisian paradox.'

As the Bishop recalls, Lewis' transfer from Oxford to Cambridge was an outstanding success – the effect on the 'mellow little college' that was Magdalene was immediate and stimulating.

The enthusiasm of Bishop Barrington-Ward as a young Chaplain is infectious and is typical of the sense of occasion which a meeting with Lewis generated.

C.S. Lewis' decision to accept an invitation to Cambridge was regarded by many friends as something of an upheaval in his life. They need not have worried: he was an immediate and outstanding success.

Bishop Simon sent me this recollection of Lewis' first footings in Cambridge and particularly at Magdalene College - it says every-thing.

'It was a halcyon time in which to be Chaplain at Magdalene. Undergraduates packed into Chapel and to meetings which I organised and I interviewed every under-graduate on his arrival in the College. Amongst the Fellowship, it was clear that this was very definitely a Christian College, and most of them came to Chapel, as many of them do to this day in that College. It was for this reason that C.S. Lewis coming from Oxford during the week to occupy his newly made Cambridge professorship, loved Magdalene, Cambridge and had a quite different relationship to Magdalen, Oxford. For many of us he enhanced the whole mellow-little College enormously and helped to create a framework for the mind and the imagination. He exercised there untrammelled his great gift, both in his entertaining conversation and in his sermons, papers and lectures, of evoking a moral and spiritual reality through literature and through the analysis of moral concepts.'

In this atmosphere it is not surprising that Simon Barrington-Ward found Lewis' high table conversation a really enjoyable if sometimes daunting experience: -

'He drew upon a massive knowledge of a great literary tradition of Europe. "You will remember that passage in Racine ....." I still remember his expositions of 'The Romance of the Rose' and 'The Fairy Queen'. One did get rather tired of saying, "No, I don't actually remember". And so one fell silent and he always assumed that you had the vast knowledge and enjoyment of all these works that he had himself. Interwoven with all these allusions was a profound sense of forgiveness of the play

*of the real forces of Heaven and Hell and a spiritual in-
sight and sense of spiritual reality. C.S. Lewis could take
you, as he'd grown himself, from what he regarded as the
dangers of an excited romantic imagination to genuine
spiritual realism. He had started from the Norse Sagas
and the Earthly Paradise. He was able to explore three
worlds, the common sense world, the world of the gods
become magic and of fairyland, and the revealed world
of moral and spiritual truth He could therefore take one
from fantasy to what seemed a powerful reality. For him
Christ was the door into the real world. But in Christ we
could claim again all the glories of the literary and ideal
world of renaissance and medieval tradition.'*

But there were more informal occasions to share as Simon
remembers:

*'I enjoyed walks with him by the Cam and in the
countryside. When I objected to the flatness and dullness
of the Cambridgeshire landscape, he insisted characteristically that every landscape was good of its kind and
we should appreciate it for itself and not com*pare it with
others. He liked to stop at a pub at some point on the walk
an*d enjoy a pint. He fitted in completely into such a scene
with his bucolic appearance. One day we were walking
and saw a haystack near a village with farm workers
beside it and through some uncanny trick of the light which
I could swear only happened when I was walking with
Jack Lewis (as we used to call him) the men appeared as
tall as the haystacks. Jack noticed it immediately "The
giants have come, shall we run and tell them!" That touch
of fantasy which came into so many of his moments and*

*which were always so entertaining. He would love one to
tell him things that caught his imagination and one felt
one had hit a kind of jackpot when one did. He liked the
remark of a bed-maker at Cambridge when asked whether
she was happy. "There ain't no such thing as 'appiness,
so we just 'ave to be 'appy wivout it." He seized upon
that. How true it was.. We are in via and not in patria. It
was the kind of point that he made in 'Surprised by Joy.'
And I remember my telling an allegorical dream which
I'd had to him and he interpreting it with great zest.'*

Simon Barrington-Ward's final reflection reminds us of the
happiness which C.S. Lewis found in his short married life with Joy
- they were engaged in a partnership which worked. Those who met
the happy couple on their Irish honeymoon encountered the same
tender happiness.

FROM SIMON AND JEAN

*'The crowning happiness was when he brought Joy
over to lunch to meet us. I followed this up with a visit to
The Kilns, their house at Headington. And I enjoyed their
banter and appreciated the toughness and salty almost
severity and bleakness at times of Joy but also the fun and
kindness. She was a much tougher lady than she appears
in the films about Jack. But it was quite true to say that
she changed his life and that he did develop, as I observed,
in the way that the films describe. There was a quite new
quality about him during that time which emerged strongly
and which I saw when he was with her particularly.
It was with tremendous anguish that I said goodbye to
him and he was very affectionate to me; and when I went*

out to Nigeria, and on one occasion was raising money for a student to come to England to hospital, I received a large anonymous donation from Magdalene, which I found out afterwards had in fact come from him. That was quite typical. He could do quite a lot of good by stealth.

I know that in earlier years he had been felt to be, in an almost immature way, often rather over-bluff and coarse in his style and that he could be rude to people. I can only say that in that case he had mellowed by the time he came to Magdalene, Cambridge. It may have been that the whole ambience was appropriate for him. Whatever it was I never saw that side of him, or hardly. And certainly I saw the deepening and maturing that was coming through his relationship with Joy.'

Simon Barrington-Ward's conclusion on his friend is equally affirmative:-

'He was a man who could evoke and explore sober spiritual reality in a way which both gripped, entertained and compelled. That is what made him such a remarkable uncontemporary apologist and such a fascinating figure.'

It is an apt conclusion and it is one that would be readily shared by the Bishop's colleagues in this quartet of impressions from those who encountered Lewis in his academic environment. Three of the comments are student based and Bishop Simon's view is that of a friend and colleague. All four affirm the greatness of the man and the conclusion which Simon has drawn.

But there was more to C.S. Lewis than either Oxford or Cambridge, both of which he held in great affection. C.S.L.

was above all a man from Ireland, a man from the Province of Ulster and especially a man from the village of Strandtown in the county Down - this preparation was important for someone who believed that roots mattered. Perhaps it is all best summed up in the homely Belfast comment of approval reserved for those who have been true to their origins and which local people often apply to their own: 'He never jumped out of the bowl he was baked in.'

C.S. Lewis would have liked that - as an example of saying things in the vernacular (and would no doubt have approved of the fearless use of the preposition)! In later Chapters we turn to some of those who were involved in the 'bowl' that was Strandtown. It was, as we shall see, a bowl of many layers – but before that a few Oxford introductions arise.

CHAPTER FOUR

An Oxford Encounter with C.S. Lewis

'When did you begin to think about coming to Oxford?' That was one of C.S. Lewis' first questions to me! When I replied, 'In the barber's shop', he was visibly surprised. He was even more surprised when I told him the shop was Billy Graham's in East Belfast - providing a personal service with which Lewis and many generations of Strandtown people were well acquainted.

As so often happens, my way forward appeared by chance when one evening in 1945 on the way home from the Belfast Shipyard I stopped by to have a haircut. Awaiting my turn I began to read Picture Post, a then famous illustrated weekly. It told the story of Ernie Fisher, a miner who had gone to Oxford with the help of an adult education bursary. 'Interesting story', I thought, until a nudge from my neighbour reminded me that I was still in the barber's and that it was my turn next.

But afterwards the story lingered on and then the question: 'If a miner goes to Oxford why not a shipyard engineer?'

I soon found out that the Trades Union Congress offered scholarships for open competition among trade unionists in Britain and Ireland, based on written examination, community service record and in-depth interviews in London and Oxford. To cut the story short, I applied and was successful. The written tests proved manageable though the interviews were formidable. In fact, little time was spent on my chosen essay subject of 'A Wages Policy'.

This path to Oxford was new territory to Lewis and he was interested to learn that the focus of the London interview was on what I had done with my time to date and what sort of post-war future did I envisage. He approved of this approach as a screening for university applications and thought it might be more widely used. He smiled when he heard my reply to the last question at the interview: 'If you get this scholarship what would you hope to do afterwards?' The gist of my reply was: 'Back to Ireland to serve the cause from Belfast' at which the Oxford don, (I heard later it was Professor A. J. P. Taylor) murmured, 'Mr. Bleakley, you recall that Gladstone's mission was to pacify Ireland and you know what happened to him!' Actually my knowledge of Gladstone was slight, but I had the wit to reply 'I take the point.'

A few days later I was awarded a scholarship of £250 a year with £3 a week during vacations. After seven years with wires and switches and a sharing in shipyard fellowship I was turning to books and lectures for a while. For me it was the chance of a lifetime which I have never regretted taking and have never undervalued. My visit to Billy Graham's barber's shop had been for me one of life's defining moments.

As I subsequently discovered, C.S. Lewis ,who took a holistic view of student care, was fascinated by such details and the way in which by very different routes we could arrive at the same destination. Nor did be underestimate the importance of having been employed in Harland and Wolff's shipyard. He knew the place well and from an early age had been in contact through trips to the 'Yard' with his grandfather, Richard. And, of course, he and Warnie had daily eye and ear contact with H & W from their attic window in 'Little Lea' and heard, with the rest of us, the 7.30 a.m. call-to-work-signal of the H & W sirens. When Lewis praised the shipyard as a great 'University of Life' and 'a considerable preparation' for higher education I began to appreciate his lack of regard for the English Public School system and his interest in the burgeoning adult education moment which students like myself represented.

Indeed, wartime and post-war Lewis put great energy into his lecturing programmes to the armed forces and developed considerably his opportunities for popular writing and broadcasting. As I learned by experience, he had something of a soft spot for those who had come to Oxford the 'hard way' and appreciated the privilege - equally he was impatient with students (for example John Betjeman) who frittered away their time.

Ruskin College, to which I belonged, was of considerable interest to Lewis and he was pleased to learn that many of us knew of his work. Then, as now, the American lobby was strong and we were fortunate in having in our College Jimmy Tyrie, an American student who was well versed in things in the world of Lewis. Jimmy was for me a boon companion on many a lecturing outing to Magdalen or the Schools to bear the great man. As he put it: 'Wait till I go back to the States and tell them I've actually heard C.S. Lewis with my own ears!' Together we managed to get our hero to the College from time to time, so that others could benefit from his wisdom.

Professor Lionel Elvin our Principal, a distinguished adult educationist and separated from Lewis' birthday by less than a decade, wrote to me recently reminding me of those days. He offers evidence of Lewis' willingness to 'go the extra mile' in helping Ruskin College students. Frank Quinn is an example: he took Frank under his wing and prepared him for a successful application as a Lecturer at Haverford College in Pennsylvania. Further evidence of Lewis' generosity comes in Lionel Elvin's comment:

> *'Frank was of a Catholic background, but had no religion himself and said to Lewis that this would hardly commend him to a Quaker College. Lewis replied: "You talk about English Literature - if the question of religion arises leave that to me."*

As my Principal, a much valued correspondent who shares my admiration for Lewis, observes, this typically positive action on behalf of Frank Quinn was 'very much to his credit.'

Equally to Lewis' credit was the special effort he made to keep in touch with his homeland and especially Ulster and the County Down; much help was given to those from home who sought his advice. To be from Strandtown was of course, to be deemed special. Surprised By Joy was not yet written, but for all who knew Lewis , there was no need to have his regard for his home heath confirmed in an autobiography. His love for a whole range of things Ulster and Irish was an obvious and important side to his personality. But, and this is a point to be stressed, he saw no tension about being Oxbridge and being Irish; love of Oxford, and later Cambridge did not lessen attachment to the homeland. Such dual loyalties were easily combined and regularly demonstrated.

As principal Elvin told each intake, we were up at Oxford for a few years of academic life which would open up new horizons. He was enthusiastic and idealistic and pointed to an opportunity to enjoy every minute of it. It was the sort of advice which Lewis himself often passed on.

These attitudes were exactly in line with my expectations. For myself, I could hardly believe my good fortune. Grant-aided to read, write, think and enjoy the society that is Oxford! 'How, compared with industrial life, can they call this work?' I thought, as we were launched on our course of studies. Years earlier C.S. Lewis had shared a similar elation with his father.

As with Lewis in the 1920s, the late 1940s was an exciting time to be in Oxford. In the immediate post-war years it was filled with students of my own age whose desire for higher education had been both interrupted and stimulated by the war. Future 'names' were generously sprinkled around the Colleges: Margaret Thatcher (née Roberts), Tony Benn, Robert Runcie, Kenneth Tynan and Ludovic Kennedy, to name but a few. Ruskin, too, had its prospective panel of 'futures': MPs and Cabinet Ministers galore, trade union leaders, industrial relations professors, high-ranking African leaders, including a future Prime Minister of Sierra Leone. For Lewis and his teaching colleagues the challenge was formidable.

Anxious as we were to get down to the books and catch up on the lost years of the war, there was a still 'rich-beyond-the-college' Oxford to explore. Everyone, poet, politician or preacher was catered for. Ruskinites majored in many of the best debating encounters at the Oxford Union and our own College Hall. Selections included political personalities as diverse as C. E. M. Joad, Harold Laski, Professor Bernal, Clement Attlee, and Christian apologists like C.S. Lewis, Donald Soper and the Master of Balliol, A.D. Lindsay.

During my first term at Ruskin College I had the opportunity to make contact with many whose fame I had known of only through their books. On one occasion I even had to contact George Bernard

Shaw on behalf of our student body. Being a fellow Irishman carried no weight whatsoever! All I received was one of his famous 'no can do' postcards with his spidery writing and radically coloured ink.

But as I found out to my lasting benefit not all Irishmen were as elusive as Shaw. The special chance encounter, which meant much to me then and more so in later years, was with one of Ulster's most famous literary sons. Ordering a coffee one morning in the popular 'Cadena' student cafe in Oxford's Cornmarket, I was interrupted by someone putting a hand on my shoulder and saying, 'What part of Belfast gave you that accent?' Looking up I saw a farmer-like man in sports coat and 'cords', who asked the question in what was clearly an Ulster accent. I told him where I came from and immediately he said, 'That's not far from where I live'. He was very interested to learn of my shipyard-to-university translation and before he left suggested that I might drop in to see him sometime in the College where he worked. 'Magdalen' he said, 'though these odd-English pronounce it ' "Maudlin" '. He continued, 'Just call in at the gate-lodge and ask for C.S. Lewis.' The name rang a bell from home but not very loudly.

Later that night at dinner Lionel Elvin, himself an English Literature scholar, put me right: 'David, my dear fellow, that's one of Oxford most interesting men; do go and see him'. I did and was always indebted for the wise advice.

We met at Magdalen from time to time (sometimes with Kenneth Tynan, one of his favourite, but often, teased students) C.S. was easy to talk to and I was privileged to experience the skill of a great communicator, who got at the spiritual heart of things in language simple but memorable. Good Ulsterman as he was, a spade was a spade and not an agricultural implement.

But better than Magdalen were the times we shared the journey back to our near-to-each-other Headington home bases. They were occasions for a cornucopia of phrases, questions and insights sufficient for a lifetime's reflection. Lewis was known to his friends as an active and lively man who loved to walk and talk, expanding on his ideas as he went along. His seemingly 'out of the blue' remarks could be startling and revealing; I share a few, illustrative of his many moods.

Sometimes he could be puckish with the questions he asked. Walking together up Headington Hill one evening this great lover of both Oxford and the County Down, turned to me, feigning a need for advice: "David, could you define Heaven for me?" I tried - he soon interrupted my theological meanderings. "My friend, you're far too complicated; an honest Ulsterman should know better. Heaven is Oxford lifted and placed in the middle of the County Down."

Not bad, not bad indeed. I am sorry that I was not then better prepared to appreciate more fully this true son of my native county, but ever since I have become aware of how much C.S. Lewis 'country' we have to explore in Ireland. Lewis left an enduring and much appreciated mark on all who knew him and I was no exception. Years later I felt a fellow feeling when Simon Barrington-Ward, Bishop of Coventry, shared with me the joy he felt on discovering that he, Simon, had been given a spiritually jovial mention in one of his hero's books.

On other occasions our exchanges had to do with things back home. C.S.L. never tired of hearing about the 'goings on' in Strandtown and district. I, for my part, was fascinated by the opportunity to see my home scene through the eyes of one who, until I came to Oxford, I regarded as very much part of Ulster's ruling class - a 'scion of the Big House' as many of his colleagues and contemporaries regarded him. But neither got it right: Lewis really did enjoy a 'rubbing of shoulders' with his 'fellow villagers' of Strandtown and was happy to contribute to a common agenda and discuss it openly.

Fortunately I was well supplied with home news and Lewis was glad to be made aware of the local gossip. My source of information was ample, for each week I received in the post from my Godmother an envelope of cuttings from the Belfast Telegraph and other regional papers more than enough to keep us in touch. Mrs. Bradshaw, who was the sender, became quite a favourite with Lewis . 'Have you got any more clippings from your Godmother', he would ask and was disappointed when they were not available. Warnie was anxious to have them as well.

At first I was surprised by his interest, but later I understood and appreciated the importance he placed on the everyday episodes which shape much of what we do and who we are. When I asked the reason why, he said that he just liked to know what was going on at grass-roots in his own green fields of Ulster, without having to await the more leisurely written letters from Gundreda, Kelsie or other members of the Ewart circle. I never associated C.S. Lewis with being an avid reader of newspapers generally, but certainly he liked being kept up-to-date with Mrs. Bradshaw's weekly clippings.

Arthur Greeves, of course, remained his long-term source of what was happening at home - but this correspondence was never discussed.

From these episodes I felt that Lewis really did believe that a 'bit of trivia' was good for the soul - back again to G. K. Chesterton's 'divinely ordinary' things. Equally, he believed that the source should be home-based, because it represented a significant microcosm of 'real people in real-life situations'.

Other memories gathered from our peripatetic discussions had to do with tips about how to go about the world of learning. These were no formal seminars - even better, they were the application of a magnificent common-sense to matters of scholarship and on the gleaning of everyday knowledge.

On reading suggestions his range was wide though sometimes I had to give up trying to keep pace with the flood of advice! (Years later I was comforted when Simon Barrington-Ward had the same experience when sharing in 'Lewis-led' High Table exchanges at Magdalen College, Cambridge!). But on popular 19th Century literature C.S.L. was most helpful, most enthusiastic and delighted to know that organisations like the Workers' Educational Association were doing much to develop literary studies. He approved of my regard for Trollope (much involved in Irish affairs), the Brontes, George Eliot, Thackery and Jane Austen; and was delighted to know that they had a considerable following in Belfast adult education circles. I was disappointed that he could not be drawn on Helen Waddell whose 'star' was high and with whom he had much in common. Helen was a great favourite back home, where she was held in high esteem at Queen's University by noted medieval scholar, Professor G. O. Sayles.

A surprise for me on one of our literary exchanges was to learn that he and I shared a favourite novel in Jane Austen's Pride and Prejudice. 'How often have you read it?' he asked. I replied 'Many times'. 'Splendid' he said and proceeded to advise me not to be afraid to read a good book 'time and time again'. He assured me that he 'dipped into' his favourites regularly and particularly Pride and Prejudice. About Jane Austen's classic I often wondered how far he (perhaps unconsciously) saw parallels between the characters and action of the plot and his own complex social life: Rosings for Glenmachan, Mr.Bennett for Papy, Elizabeth for Joy, and so on.

But whichever of the many topics were under discussion C.S.L. was ever anxious to warn against looking for a complicated explanation when none was required. He was especially impatient with those who discarded the plain common-sense for the complex. Amusingly on one occasion he took to task those who read deep meaning into his smoking habits and his attachment to a collection of favourite pipes:

> *'They wonder why I like to smoke a pipe and think it has something to do with getting me into a contemplative frame of mind. Do they never consider that I might just like the taste and smell of tobacco!'*

I was no smoker, so our most shared consumption was not tobacco but tea. We consumed gallons of the brew together and agreed that 'no cup was big enough' to satisfy our thirst for Ulster's favourite beverage. He appreciated (without endorsing!) my quotation of a popular temperance slogan: 'Ulster would be a better place if the men passed more pubs and fewer resolutions!'

But sometimes C.S.L. could be very serious during an exchange. On one rare occasion when by chance we got on to family matters, he asked me casually about my mother and father. I had much to say about my father, a bricklayer, who had brought our family up in a radical tradition and who, like many of his generation had sacrificed much for the sake of others. He had been proud to see me go to Oxford and promised to keep the home going until my return. Looking pensive for a moment, Lewis said I was lucky to have such a firm relationship and that I ought to value it. I have since wondered whether he had his own father in mind.

Then he broached a question which I have never forgotten and to which he never returned: 'What about your mother, has she helped, too?' I hesitated and then explained: 'My mother is dead; she died shortly after my birth; a matter of weeks.'

My companion and mentor was silent for a long moment and then asked a question which I have often pondered: 'Which, my friend, is the greater loss to bear - to be separated from your mother when only a few weeks have gone or when nearly a decade has passed?'

Fifty years later I'm still trying to work that one out. Never again did we discuss our parents with each other and I knew that we would not. We had been given a fortuitous and once-for-all opportunity to delve into a filial matter of common concern. Hopefully we were each strengthened by the occasion. I relate it because, of all the many times we shared thoughts, this was by far the closest and most human exchange.

On academic subjects we had not much in the way of overlap. Medieval literary studies and languages were beyond me though I had some advantage, especially by practical experience, where industrial relations and economics were concerned. So inevitably many of our 'walking home' discussions had to do with the Attlee Labour Government's efforts to copper-bottom the Welfare State or, as mischievous Oxford critics sometimes dubbed it, 'The Farewell State'. I found C.S.L. in many ways a traditionalist, but he was no reactionary. His acquaintance with Shaw, Wells and Chesterton had given him a generous social vision; he even occasionally hinted that there might be a Fabian skeleton or two in the Irish family cupboard.

However, he tended to keep party politics at a distance and I was no exception. My own stance as a Christian Socialist and pacifist in the R. H. 'Tawney-Keir Hardie tradition' was of no avail. I suspected that he preferred total abstention to perfect moderation where the art of politics was concerned. However, I could hardly fault his final advice: 'Take it to the Lord in prayer, but pray carefully lest your prayers are answered'.

Fortunately I never had to canvass C.S. Lewis for his vote, but Arthur Greeves I did canvass. To the best of my knowledge I never 'made it' into his 'Letters to Lewis', so I shall never know his voting pattern. However, as I canvassed I always hoped (and flattered myself) that perhaps I may, at least, have persuaded him to abstain!

The truth of the matter is that Lewis was too diverse a man to accept the traditional confines of any one political party though I often regretted that he was not closer to Oxford's leading Christian Socialist of the time, A. D. Lindsay, Master of Balliol. Lindsay did so much to raise the sights of a post-war generation. He enthused us with his conviction that we had 'to combine goodness and cleverness' so as 'to harness the scientific mind in the service of the merciful heart'. I always felt that these Christian philosophers had much in common on what is still a crucial issue as we prepare for a new millennium, hopefully drawing on visionaries like these two from Oxford.

Lewis was very much a 'conscience of the community' man and was even-handed in his advice to the contending political establishments. So much so that when in 1951 he was offered a well earned CBE by Winston Churchill he refused the distinction. The refusal caused quite a stir and many from opposing party political wings pleaded with him to accept the honour. But Lewis was firm. He let it be known that though on a purely personal level the honour would be 'highly agreeable', he feared that acceptance would play into the hands of 'knaves' who accused him of 'covert anti-leftist propaganda' in his religious writings and of 'fools' who believed the accusations. Many of us who were neither knaves nor fools, tried to persuade him to reconsider, but he remained firm in his refusal. We respected his motives.

Nevertheless, Lewis never 'short changed' on his community obligations; his extra-mural services were considerable. During the First World War he had felt it his obligation to 'join up' and during the Second War he became a member of the local Home Guard in

Oxford. He also opened his home for the reception of evacuees and showed an immense capacity to adapt to the pressures of wartime civilian life. Not being a car driver was an added inconvenience which often turned him into something of a ' beast of burden' in the transport of domestic supplies for Mrs. Moore. At times his overladen bicycle looked like one of those encountered in an African outback.

Lewis' vast correspondence was another 'extra' willingly given and in its own way provided a social service of advice to thousands far and wide. Indeed many an MP or town Councillor would have regarded the throughput as considerable - all this on top of committees and public lecturing occasions galore. Little wonder that he felt little need to join up with a political party in order to 'do his bit' for society.

However he was very tolerant to those who felt otherwise and had friends across the political spectrum. His students knew this and benefited from his breadth of vision. I, too, was a beneficiary.

Years later I was reminded once again of his generosity of spirit. It happened like this. During one of C.S. Lewis' visits to his beloved County Down with Joy, his wife, and when I had become a Member of Parliament in East Belfast: (covering 'Little Lea', 'Bernagh' and 'Ty-Isa' as well), I took my friend on a fleeting car trip to the nearby Parliament Building which he had yet to see. After a quick tour of our legislative centre we stood on the steps of Parliament, overlooking the splendour of the County Down and his evocative Castlereagh Hills. We looked hard and long at all our surroundings; and we shared reflections on the 'then' of Oxford and the 'now' of our native Ulster and the County Down.

It was a magic moment, during which C.S.L. seemed to relent where I was concerned and showed acceptance and enthusiasm for my political commitment. I felt that all was forgiven as he, with a jovial wave of his hands in a double benediction to both Parliament Buildings behind us and the County Down vista before us, proclaimed: 'David, my friend, you've really made it. Look behind and before you: all this and Heaven, too.'

'What a satisfactory conclusion', I thought, as I drove my favourite mentor back to 'The Old Inn at Crawfordsburn'.

CHAPTER FIVE

Cowley Fathers –
A Monastic Experience

C.S. Lewis was normally a very outgoing person but, as was also well-known, there were areas of his private life which he preferred to keep entirely to himself. This was especially so in spiritual matters. For example as Walter Hooper, who has a uniquely sensitive knowledge of his teacher and friend , once reminded me 'there were many sides of Lewis' religious life about which the world knew nothing.'

Like his father, 'he did good by stealth and blushed to find it fame.'

Equally private, and often quite unknown to outsiders, was C.S. Lewis' involvement with the Oxford based Society of St. John the Evangelist which, from 1940, opened up for him the opportunity of weekly Confession. His Spiritual Director was an Anglican, Father Walter Adams, who lived at the Society's centre in Cowley, not far from Magdalen College.

It was my good fortune, and quite by chance, to become aware of Lewis' links with the Society. Ultimately from within the Fellowship of St. John I was able to appreciate something of his interaction with the 'Cowley Fathers' (as they were often called) and what it meant to him and the Order.

It came about like this. On one of our back-to-home discussion opportunities I happened to mention that back in Belfast there was growing interest in the linkage between society and religion. Boldly I proclaimed that all my upbringing and all my instincts suggested to me that there must be a linkage. I even quoted Keir Hardie (for whose place in social history Lewis had considerable respect) and his Isaiah vision of the Kingdom of God on earth.

Kindly, and patient as ever, Lewis did not demur - instead he pointed out that there was a special place of contemplation and social outreach in Oxford, run by the Society of St. John the Evangelist. He spoke highly of their work and witness in Britain and further afield; they had a strong sense of social purpose; they were Anglicans and very much involved in the world about. 'You should pay them a visit' - he said.

And so I did. I decided to make my own contact and one night turned up for Evensong at the Society's monastery (they preferred to call it 'Mission House') at 16 Marston Street. There I met the Guest Master, Christopher Bryant, one of the Society's greatest thinkers - it was to mean for me a lifelong association and an opening of fellowship within the wider national and international Church. My fellow pilgrim, true to his standards of spiritual privacy did not ever seek to monitor my progress within the Society; the rule with the Cowley Fathers was and is a golden one, 'to observe but never to obtrude'. I remain forever grateful to the great spiritual 'Navigator' who pointed me in the right direction and the Society which accepted me.

Since then as one of its Trustees I have been deeply involved in the affairs of the Society and am regularly in residence in one of its

Houses in London or Oxford. My wife and I enjoy the opportunity of sharing our County Down home with the Society as a base for their regular peacemaking visits to our Province. So C.S.L's preparing of the way for me within S.S.J.E. continues to bear fruit. He would approve of S.S.J.E.'s current links with Bangor and other parts of our land.

The Society of St. John the Evangelist with which C.S. Lewis became associated in 1940 was founded at Oxford in 1886 by Father Richard Benson - and it was the first religious community for men to be established in the Church of England since the Reformation. The foundation standards were high and have been well maintained. The aim was that the whole of life should be orientated towards God, always bearing in mind the changing conditions and demands of a rapidly changing world. In practical terms, today, that means open and well- ordered worship, links with education, arts and science, social outreach and personal counselling services.

These activities add up to what Father Christopher Bryant, a great admirer of Lewis, once called "The Search for God in Depth." For Christopher Bryant, monastic peace brought a tranquillity of order enabling us to learn to accept our destiny. In other words, through self-knowledge, through prayer, mediation and contemplation, it becomes possible to cooperate with God and to grow to full human stature.

Looking back, I can appreciate more fully why Lewis , and indeed many of my generation, were attracted to an oasis for contemplation such as S.S.J.E. in the 1940s. It was a time when we were looking for post-war personal guidelines to take us into "What's it all about?" questions which tug at every soul and with which we were constantly confronted at countless University seminars. As Lewis clearly recognised, a battle was going on for possession of the souls of those who were being called upon to build a new world order. So we needed sustenance for the encounter - Screwtape was about!

C.S. Lewis had never any doubt about the relevance of the monastic contribution to the modern scene. For him these monks had an approach to religion and a life style that made sense of a muddled world with its manifold contradictions which bear hard on much of God's creation. Basically a man of simple tastes and needs, he was at home with a religious community that encouraged members to treat possessions as a trust from God and to practise moderation in eating and drinking. In addition, avoidance of excessive expense on dress and amusements is regarded as an opportunity for self-discipline in daily life and witness.

'A tough regime' the world might say. But not really - in everyday life benchmarks are helpful guides to action. Indeed, most monastic rules are little more than formal language for pretty sensible patterns of behaviour which make life more manageable and, above all, more meaningful.

There were many, of course, who found Lewis' link with a monastic establishment a bit out of character, especially coming from an Ulsterman who was expected to view with suspicion the rather High Church traditions of the Cowley Fathers. But, in fact, in his embrace of S.S.J.E. C.S. Lewis was responding to something deeply embedded in Christian Ireland and in the best traditions of St. Patrick. Coming, as he did from the County Down, Lewis was well placed to appreciate Oxford's Cowley Fathers. From his favourite town of Bangor and the Abbey which he regarded with affection the tramp of Irish monks has been heard across Europe for 1500 years - France, Germany, Switzerland, Austria, Italy and even further afield; their presence was felt as they came not to colonise but to save. C.S.L would have approved of Cardinal Tomas O'Fiaich's reference to

Columbanus as 'the first European' - a contemporary recognition that monasticism has for long sought a balance behind and beyond the cloister.

So, far from acting out of character, Lewis was reasserting an historic allegiance forged in the land of his birth by founders of the Faith.

And of considerable importance, because or his high profile by entering into fellowship with the Cowley Fathers he was also contributing to the demystification of monasteries and convents - a development which would make it more possible for monks and nuns to share their life style and insights with the outside world. Though he did not advertise his link with S.S.J.E., neither did he deny it. So Lewis became a symbol of change for many who were looking anew at religious Orders.

Of course for some people monastic life is all a bit of a mystery, and the popular image of monks remains a caricature. Outsiders still wonder what goes on behind monastery and convent walls. Indeed sometimes the media and the world at large seem to watch in fascinated anticipation for someone to 'leap over the wall' and tell what it's all about. I often wonder what they expect to find and no doubt so did CSL. My own experience is of professing men and women reflecting life in all its rich variety. Like the rest of us, with God's help, they get on with the business of coping with their daily 'ups and downs'. Nor, as Lewis discovered, were monks short on knowledge of the world. On the contrary, he was struck by the considerable pre-ordination experience in every walk of life of those in full communion, particularly in Post War II days.

Lewis may have considered his contribution to the demystification process modest, but his presence among the Cowley Fathers did not go unnoticed among the religious. A wider public was encouraged to take note and a significant increase in the number of retreats took place with a growing number of laity giving help through the supporting Fellowship of St. John (F.S.J.). 'I leap over the wall' books by Monica Baldwin, Karen Armstrong and other 'insiders' began to appear as a result of the new ferment. Since then a process of change has taken place within the closed Orders which continue to promote interchange with the secular world. C.S.L. would have protested his innocence of all this, but for those of us who played a minor role he was a notable fellow traveller.

Members of the Order have attested to the value of Lewis' presence and the added distinction it brought. He was, for instance, always willing to give talks to members and friends when called upon. Brother Anslem, had the pleasant task of greeting him when he came to the House in Marston Street, Oxford, to visit his Confessor or lecture to students. The Brother remembers him: 'A man full of life and fun. He was nothing like a University don. He always made me think of a very prosperous farmer - at least his build made me think of that. He had great contacts all over the place.' The late Fr. Christopher Bryant, one of S.S.J.E's most outstanding leaders, valued Lewis as 'one of our greatest spiritual writers' and he in turn returned the compliment. Occasionally these two remarkable men had an opportunity to meet at the Society's House, Dean's Yard, Westminster. What a pity their discussions were not recorded for posterity.

C.S. Lewis' involvement with S.S.J.E. extended beyond using the Community home as a place of worship though, in fact, he often worshipped in the Chapel when his duties at Magdalen permitted. No one was all that surprised to know that Lewis was attending daily worship, but surprise was registered among his inner circle of friends when in the closing months of 1940 he began the practice of weekly confession. Not many, in fact, knew of the development; as was the Rule, members of the Order kept the knowledge of such personal witness within the walls of the monastery. All of which invites the conclusion that Lewis saw his decision in 1940 to seek a spiritual director as a somewhat gradual but very normal part of a pilgrimage begun in 1929, when shortly before the death of his father, he recognised that God was God. In view of the time lapse he cannot be accused of hurrying things.

The period around 1940 was an unsettling one for Lewis and it was a good moment to reassess his spiritual resources and needs. All around him at this time were uncertainties: worries about a far from well Warnie who had been sent on military service to France; the fear of invasion underlined by Churchill's 1940 call for a sacrifice of 'blood, toil, tears and sweat'; the reminder of the need to take up arms by service in the Home Guard; and his increasing involvement in wartime debates, bringing him into conflict with pacifist groups, which included many close friends. All in all, the additional pressure on Lewis was great and the decision to accept the discipline of weekly confession provided him with what seemed a unique framework of certainty, appropriate to his needs.

Yet there were still doubts: 'What will they think of me at home?'; 'Am I doing this for the good of my soul or to placate my ego?'; 'Is this well thought out or is it an emotional spasm?' Questions such as these were likely to assail Lewis in what was then a much disturbed personal life. But never one for self-pity he decided to 'plunge in'; and plunge in he did by accepting Father Walter Adams, a noted priest from S.S.J.E. as his spiritual director. It was a true meeting of very different but very saintly minds. From the first meeting Lewis warmed to his director and before long was describing him as the most holy man he had ever met. When he died in 1952 Lewis was devastated.

As a layman, my own contact with Fr. Adams was at a distance, but his Brethren have shared their personal memories. Their recollections are warm and completely in accord with Lewis' view of his monastic guide as 'the most impressive spiritual confidant' he had ever encountered.

The Cowley Evangelist (April 1952), the journal of S.S.J.E., gives a good picture of the man and priest who met with Lewis on a regular basis for some twelve years:-

> *'Of your charity pray for the Repose of the Soul of Walter Frederick Adams, Mission Priest of the Society of St. John the Evangelist, who passed to his rest on Monday, March 3, at Headington, Oxford, in the eighty-second year of his age, and thirty-sixth year of his religious profession.*
>
> *His father was a priest; and after studying at Keble College, Oxford, and Wells Theological College, he was ordained in 1897; and after serving in two curacies, he came to our Society and was professed in 1916. From 1921 to 1927 he was in Africa, chiefly at St. Cuthbert's Mission; and later he had one year in Bombay. The rest of his professed life he spent almost entirely at Oxford. He was a great conductor of retreats all over the country and was much liked as a preacher; but quite the most remarkable feature of his ministry, especially in his later years, was his capacity for helping individual souls as a confessor and director. A countless multitude of people found in him an unfailing source of strength and encouragement. He had a keen sense of humour and a great love of souls. He was described in the obituary notice in the <u>Church Times</u> as "one of the best-loved mission priests of the S.S.J.E.", and this is indeed true.'*

Lewis had known Fr. Adams by repute and by all accounts he had made a careful choice in his confessor and director. All who knew Adams knew of his unique ability to 'get through' to his charges and to win and maintain their confidence. No easy task in view of the high calibre penitents who came his way. Fortunately he had a keen sense of humour with a capacity for understanding. He deserved his accolade from the <u>Church Times</u> one of 'the best-loved' priests in the Society. From others who knew Fr. Adams, I have gleaned the following about this holy man who guided Lewis spiritually through some of the most vital years of his life - years which saw him at the peak of his powers as a Christian apologist. Joy, charity, sympathy, wisdom tempered with a gaiety that never left him - these are the themes that are underlined.

A lady, who is but one of a great company of his spiritual children, writes:

> '*He never spared himself, and always made you feel how much he loved you. He just radiated love and joy, and was always talking of it; and he has helped me to love our Lord far more than I had ever done before. As he grew older, I think his Retreat addresses became more and more spiritual. It was all so natural and simple and so real to him.*'

Fr. O'Brien, who, as Superior, knew him well, wrote:

> '*He had a special gift for disordered souls, a tireless patience, and a quite unflagging zeal for their spiritual needs. But also his stimulating and vitalizing energy attracted people of all sorts. His great accessibility and ready friendline were a great help to him in his ministry.*'

He brought new hope and courage into many despondent souls. As a preacher and conductor of retreats he was in constant request.'

And from C.S. Lewis himself, writing of one who was twenty-seven years his senior and very much a trusted father figure, this tribute:

'To me he meant a great deal. Indeed in all the years in which he was both my spiritual director and close friend I have met no one from whom I have derived so much help and counsel, and whose companionship I have valued so highly. He was, I think you will agree, in many ways unique. He had a most profound knowledge of humanity. His judgements were penetrating and at the same time sympathetic. I am sure the secret was the great love which he had for our Lord which illumined his relations with men. When he was at the height of his powers, his preaching was original and arresting. The fact that his sermons did not read well is indicative of how much depended on the personality of the preacher himself. Beside all this he was musical and he had a delightful sense of humour.'

This is high praise, indeed, and brings out the totality of Fr. Adams' outreach and his uniqueness in his field as a counsellor. For Lewis his great personal dependence on Adams is manifest and there is a richness of thankfulness in his affirmation that 'I have met no one from whom I have derived so much help and counsel and whose companionship I have valued so highly.'

This is a measure of how much Lewis was to lose as he faced what he did not know would be the last decade of his life without his beloved spiritual director.

Lewis lamented the loss of his spiritual director in 1952 and lament he might.

He had built up a special relationship of confidence which made him the recipient of trusted advice on which he had come to rely. That fellowship with a very saintly man had given Lewis a stability which was invaluable during what was one of the most creative periods in his life. He was never to find another Fr. Adams.

So the 1950s became for Lewis a very lonely period when he was essentially on his own in a whole series of 'crunch' situations. To the outside world it might not have seemed so as honourific rewards came his way: C.B.E. (refused), honours from a host of universities and election to The British Academy to name only a few. But such gestures, well-intentioned and well earned, are often a real encumbrance to those who are at the peak of their powers in their chosen field. Certainly they did little to help Lewis in dealing with practical and fundamental upsets in his everyday life which only he could deal with and in which a soulmate is often indispensable. We have already recorded the passing of Fr. Adams, but there were other blows. In the previous year Mrs. Moore had also died and so an important link with his formative years was severed. Warnie, too, brother and closest of companions continued his battle against alcohol. Lewis was never sure what form the latest crisis might take and whether he might have to travel to Co. Louth in Ireland or call on local medical intervention. Practical problems such as these proved a heavy drain on Lewis' time and energy in the 1950s. There was also a burden involved in the transfer from Magdalen, Oxford to Magdalene College, Cambridge. True there was great rejoicing in Cambridge and particularly in his new College, but for Lewis the honour had come late in life and involved him in travelling and other domestic adjustments which were an additional burden in an already complicated life style. 'Dashing about' was not a comfortable pursuit for one who had health problems which required a leisurely life style. The Fathers at S.S.J.E. commented on this practical aspect of things and were protective of him.

Then for a few years it seemed that all might work out - C.S. Lewis had found his soulmate. In 1956 and 1957 the world became aware when Helen Joy Davidman Gresham and Clive Staples Lewis were married, first in Oxford's Registry Office and later by the Rev. Peter Bide in the local hospital. Tragically this marriage between Jack and Joy, which seemed so perfect to all who shared their company, was to be of short duration. They lived their partnership to the full and Joy's children were encircled in their love, but after considerable suffering Joy died on 13 July, 1960: the little family, Warnie, Jack and his two stepchildren were left to bear the pain.

For C.S. Lewis there was no Father Adams to whom he could turn, but, as his shortly-to be written **A Grief Observed** made clear, he had been given inner spiritual resources which he shared with others in similar circumstances. It was a tremendous effort and a fitting tribute to his old friend and confessor. Ever since, it has become a source of comfort to all who lose their soulmate.

A POSTSCRIPT ON FATHER ADAMS AND THE MANNER OF HIS PASSING

C.S. Lewis had a profound regard for his confessor and when Father Adams died in 1952 he shared his grief with many of his friends.

He came to believe that his aged confessor had died while celebrating at the altar - he was probably confusing the occasion with an earlier incident in the history of the Society. Whatever the explanation, the version believed by Lewis in 1952 soon became the accepted account of Father Adams' last hours on earth. Since then it has been much printed and often quoted.

Some time ago, while going through the Oxford records of S.S.J.E., I read an account of the occasion by Father Dalby, then Superior General of the Society. It was clear from this account that Father Adams had not died at the Altar nor even in Church. In fact, surrounded by his brethren, he died in a quite domestic setting. The present Superior General of the Society, Father James Naters, has since confirmed this version.

I share a letter which I have received from Fr. Naters. It comments on the life and work of Fr. Adams and gives an account of his passing on 3 March, 1952

22 Great College Street,
Westminster,
London

Dear David,

Thank you for your letter, asking about our Father Walter Adams, who was confessor to C.S. Lewis .

Father Adams died quietly and peacefully on March 3rd 1952, in the evening. The last months of his life were spent in sickness due to a recurrence of sprue contracted many years before in India. Fr. Adams was looked after and nursed by two friends in their house at Headington. Great joy and a lively gaiety marked his spirit, and this continued to the end. He laid down his life very quietly, with no struggle or pain. I remember the day of Fr. Adams' death very well, for I had that day arrived at Cowley and I was admitted as a postulant at Compline that evening. News came of the death of Fr. Adams, and so after Compline, about 10 p.m., Fr. Francis Dalby, the Supe-

rior, went up to Headington to the house where Fr. Adams had just died.

Accounts of Fr. Adams dying while celebrating Holy Communion are sheer fantasy.

Yours very sincerely,
James Naters S.S.J.E., Superior.
18 February, 1997.

NOTE BY DAVID BLEAKLEY, AUGUST 1998

The small bit of research involved in this incident brings to mind the excellent library and study facilities which have been a feature of S.S.J.E. work since its inception. Members of the Order and friends of the Society have made good use of the facilities and have shared their resources with a wider community.

Not all pieces of research have been as simple as this, but I can believe that C.S. Lewis and Father Adams are enjoying our earthly confusion.

No doubt they are in complete agreement and would have us remember - what matters most is how you die and not <u>where</u> you expire!

CHAPTER SIX

Lewis Genesis -
an Irish Preparation

The land that C.S. Lewis was born into in 1898 had been England's oldest colony for most of modern history; since 1169 there had been a long and often tragic colonial experience. Try as they might, the colonial rulers could not pacify Ireland; nor could they truly unite it. By the time of Lewis' birth the island, though deemed to be one administratively, was deeply divided culturally and politically. The long debated 'two islands one state' vision of relations between London and Dublin was once again up for discussion with demands for fundamental revision being made in influential circles in both Capitals. C.S. Lewis' early years were affected by the dispute.

But it was never going to be easy. Gladstone, who had once pledged to 'pacify Ireland' was also the author of the exasperated remark: 'Just when you begin to understand the Irish Question they change the Question!' During Lewis' boyhood the 'Question' was changing as never before. The new issues gave rise to communal uncertainties in the Ulster community of which he was a part and to which he felt an allegiance. But he never wavered in that allegiance; nor, like many of his fellow Irish, did he find it incompatible with his national identity. Nevertheless these were difficult questions for the young Jack growing up in an emotionally charged Province and in a home privy to the political situation. This domestic disturbance arose because father Albert often used 'Little Lea' as a political drop-in centre for his Unionist Party associates. Neither Warnie nor Jack welcomed such occasions and gave indications of being bored by the company.

C.S. Lewis, of course, was never 'home bound' even in his earliest days. He was always aware that he was a part of a wider culture and, though conscious in the early 1900s that he was witnessing history in the making, he was also intellectually aware of the Anglo-Irish culture to which he belonged and to which his people had contributed. Like many of his social class, he had much in common with his Southern counterparts. Such awareness could not be otherwise: he was an intelligent and inquisitive boy growing up in an environment which provided him with a well stocked supply of books to feed his cultural curiosity. His father's cosmopolitan personal library was at hand and his sons were encouraged to use it. Equally available and much appreciated was Belfast's famous downtown Linen Hall Library a favourite meeting place for Ulster's literary set. This library, established in 1788 was, and is, a unique centre for Irish books, local and national.

The Linen Hall Library also fulfilled the function of an informal club for scholars and writers and promoted many cultural good causes. Equally, its radical traditions attracted into membership many of the Province's most creative thinkers and philanthropists. 'The Linen Hall' (as it is known locally - called after an earlier textile foundation) was for the Lewis brothers and their father (whose legal office at 83 Royal Avenue was nearby) a favourite spot for browsing and meeting-up with one another. C.S.L. could also indulge his interest in the intellectual history of his land. The recorded wisdom of Ireland's greats provided an historical benchmark for animated discussions. Lewis was at home in such a setting and was always grateful for his father's patronage.

Ireland's intellectual giants were many and varied and like many of his contemporaries, Lewis became aware that he was part of a rich Irish tradition of scholarship and intellectual brilliance of which he could be proud. Nor were these 'greats' parochial - their influence stretched far beyond the Irish 'parish' as Lewis was to note with pride when he encountered Oxford.

Not surprisingly, Edmund Burke (1729-1797) was high on his list. It could not be otherwise in the historic library setting where Burke's Reflections on the Revolution in France had been discussed at length by the Belfast intelligensia during the revolution of 1789 - a year after the founding of the Linen Hall. Lewis admired, in particular, Burke's command of words and his masterly use of the art of the 'pithy observation'. One of C.S.L.'s own pithy remarks about the great political philosopher and orator was 'he is eminently quotable'. He retained an interest in Burke throughout his life and often recommended his merit when advising reading programmes. We shared an admiration for Edmund Burke; unfortunately we never **did** get round to discussing Tom Paine's famous riposte!

Lewis had also great respect for Bishop George Berkeley (1685-1753), a prolific writer on social philosophy and who with Swift and others was part of a brilliant society of Irish thinkers of his time. From an early date in his reading career Lewis was impressed with Berkeley's work and advised Arthur Greeves to follow his example. Lewis thought that Berkeley was underestimated but, as in the case of Forrest Reid his Belfast writer friend, he believed that his day would come. He would have been pleased to read this Irish tribute to the Bishop (by Joseph Johnston, Bishop Berkeley's Querist, Dundalgan Press, Dundalk 1970) concerning an American tour by Ireland's energetic social philosopher: 'He made contact and established friendship with some of America's outstanding men and the Berkeley tradition, in all its civilising and humanising influence, is a living reality in that country as well as in Ireland and England'. High praise, indeed. Lewis would have approved - indeed, before he was out of his 'teens it is interesting to note that he was offering much the same judgement. Further evidence of his remarkable intellectual maturity.

Like C.S.L., Bishop Berkeley ended his career in Oxford and is buried in Christ Church. A generation earlier his fellow Irishman Robert Boyle (Boyle's Law) had also made a lasting impact on Oxford with his ability to combine scientific and theological studies. Testimonies to his greatness abound in the University.

But closer than any of these to Lewis in spirit and literary style was Jonathan Swift (1667-1745), who had links with Belfast and the Ulster Province. Like Lewis , he was interested in the literary/religious affairs of his time and their careers had many common features. His inventive skill with words, and an ability to mingle reality and make believe, enabled him to reach out to a readership which was at once intergenerational, intersocial and international. Lewis (Orwell, too, in Animal Farm writings) owed much to the inspiration of Swift and was very much a 'brother in words' with the Dean where Gulliver's Travels was concerned. In today's parlance, they were 'two of a kind', each belonging to a select league of Anglo-Irish writers.

It is also interesting to note that Swift's interest in the celebrated Scriblerus Club of his day, which brought together Pope, Congreve, Lord Oxford and other notables, was matched by the 20th century Oxford version of The Inklings. By all accounts Swift's group with its wide-ranging discussions on 'all false tastes in learning' was as ribald and irreverent in comments and conclusions as was its Oxford descendant.

So, an early looking-back into Ireland's past provided evidence for Lewis that at Oxford he would be entering into an intellectual inheritance to which his countrymen had fully subscribed. His country women had not yet been given a chance to subscribe, but when they were they acquitted themselves with distinction.

Ireland, in fact, has always made a substantial contribution to Western scholarship but, as Lewis knew, the contribution has often gone unnoticed or, as in his case, had been given an English accreditation. Hopefully this Biography will do something to turn the tide.

However, formidable 'pebbles' remain to be collected. Just recently on a visit to Killyleagh Castle, County Down, another of Lewis' 'you must see' places, I was reminded that this was the birthplace in 1660 of Hans Sloane, one of the greatest physicians and natural history collectors of his day. Sloane would certainly have qualified for Lewis' Irish scholar pantheon. Sloane's collection became the nucleus around which the British Museum was founded. When he died, he was regarded by many as the most distinguished Irish Londoner of his day. A more homely and lasting memorial to Sloane, and one well-known to Lewis, is Sloane Street in London. It is, say the local populace: 'Like Sloane's life, long and straight'.

Such encounters with Ireland's great figures of the past were vital in giving young Jack Lewis a sense of identity and confidence before he was launched into the wider world of pre-University learning.

However, so far we have been looking into the impact on Lewis of 18th and 19th Century Ireland with its great upsurge of Anglo-Irish learning. But around the time of Lewis' birth new names in national literature were beginning to appear. They were to do with a spectacular renewal of Irish literature around names like Shaw, Wilde, Joyce, O'Casey and Yeats. Here again Lewis was well placed to become familiar with the new literature. He was particularly interested in William Butler Yeats whom be was to get to know at Oxford. Shaw, too, attracted his attention and even more so, Oscar Wilde. He also had a special place in his affection for Forrest Reid, once described as 'the first Ulster novelist to achieve European status'.

I can recall his grief at Reid's passing in 1947 after a long, distinguished, but underestimated writing career in Belfast. There is a plaque to his memory on the family house, often visited by Lewis and Greeves. Indeed, Lewis, Greeves and Forrest Reid often teamed up on Co. Down outings.

However, this inflow of new literature from Irish writers did not deflect Lewis from his earlier Anglo-Irish cultural affiliation. Ecumenical as he was in literature as well as religion, he could combine the best of new Ireland literature with the Anglo-Irish tradition of the past. Indeed he was willing to defend his stance to the full. He was proud of the Northern stock from which be had come and was deeply aware of the contribution which his kith and kin had made to nation and to Empire. With W. B. Yeats he was ever ready to demonstrate that the Protestants of Ireland were not a petty people. He approved of the poet's later protest to the newly formed Irish Senate in Dublin after independence was granted:

> *'We are the people of Burke; we are the people of Grattan; we are the people of Swift, the people of Emmet, the people of Parnell. We have created most of the modern literature of this country. We have created the best of its political intelligence.'*

Superbly certain and perhaps a little arrogant; but it was the kind of proclamation that added to Lewis' own certainty when he was an adolescent growing up in Belfast in the constitutional upheavals of the times. It was an important preparatory stage in his life before be was launched on his lecturing and writing career.

BELFAST INFLUENCES

But more immediate than 'all-Ireland' influences on young Jack Lewis were those which emanated from his Belfast home background during some of the most impressionable years of his life, 1910-1914. In those years Belfast became the centre for what seemed likely to become an act of rebellion against the sovereign Parliament at Westminster. Even more overpowering was the proximity of 'Little Lea' to the revolutionary activity. The pro-Union campaign was led from 'Craigavon' - stately home of Captain James Craig in whose spacious grounds some 50,000 volunteers assembled in September, 1911. They were 'sworn in' to defend the Union after a rallying call to resistance by the well-known Lord Carson of Dublin and the leader of the Unionist movement. Leafy Circular Road was transformed by such events; and so, too, were 'Little Lea' and 'Bernagh', each overlooking 'Craigavon' and within easy hearing of the demonstrations.

This Biography is not a guide book to the constitutional history of the period, but it is important to appreciate that what was happening to the Lewis brothers in their 1911 home setting would have an effect on matters to do with their life style and particularly their education and career prospects. At this time they were only 13 years and 16 years old.

For the two brothers, who had lost their mother and whose father was deeply involved in the political crisis, life at 'Little Lea' was unsettled and insecure - no wonder they depended on each other's company and that of nearby friend, Arthur Greeves. It is also important to remember that when Jack was most concerned about his schooling his home life was dominated by a father who was still distracted by the death of his wife and by growing political involvement. In such circumstances it was difficult to have in-depth discussions about future schooling. There seems to have been little real consultation with the children or close contact between father Lewis and the school authorities.

So were taken a series of extraordinary decisions with regard to education - an all-too-short acquaintance with what seemed an eminently suitable Campbell College; and then followed far from satisfactory English experiences. Happily for Jack all worked out well when eventually Wm. T. Kirkpatrick, 'The Great Knock' (originally from Ulster but then retired to Surrey) became his private and much loved tutor. Many have criticised Albert Lewis for sending his boys to England for education. It is only fair to record that boarding 'across-the-water' education for the children of wealthy Irish Protestant parents was very normal at the turn of the Century and to some extent still is. Those, in particular who were seeking a public School education were wedded to the system and of course the political instability of the time encouraged the practice.

It is also important to note that Jack, in contrast to brother Warnie, found difficulty in settling into any school chosen by father Albert. It is likely that the young C.S.L. preferred a one-to-one relationship with an out-standing tutor, plus the opportunity for extensive private study. Whatever the explanation, the English arrangement ultimately worked out for the Lewis boys and there is no clear evidence that academically they lost out in the process.

It is however obvious that the two boys felt that they had been cast off in order to facilitate their father and his preoccupation with other priorities, political in particular.

Had they but known it in nearby County Antrim a young Louis MacNeice, himself a son of the Manse, who also had lost his mother early in life, was about to be sent off to endure the loneliness of English Public School life. He died in the same year as C.S. Lewis, after a distinguished career as a poet. The isolation from Albert Lewis undoubtedly made the brothers increasingly dependent on each other (it became a lifelong dependence) and deepened the happy connection built up with their Ewart relations. It is also very probable that Lewis' reluctance to engage in party politics may have originated from these unhappy schooling arrangements. Certainly he never spoke enthusiastically about his father's political commitment. Nor did he show many signs of gratitude for what turned out to be a reasonably happy and academically successful English schooling experience. Some of his grumbling was hard to justify.

However the home influence was in evidence when the question of war service became a possibility. Each of the brothers felt that 'joining up' was a natural thing to do, even though as Irish residents they would have been excused military service should they have so indicated. But 'joining the army' to fight for King and Country was by no means unusual in Ireland, 1914-18. Indeed, some 132,000 across the island so decided, emphasising once again the ambiguity which governed relations between Dublin and Belfast and all of Ireland and Britain.

The First World War in fact defused the revolutionary strategy which was developing at 'Craigavon': suddenly the whole of Ireland, reacting to the declaration of war against Germany, perceived a need to unite against a more obvious enemy. The transformation was extraordinary as North and South in Ireland the call went out - 'Your Country and Empire need You'. Throughout Ireland those who had been preparing to wage war on one another were enjoined to fight a German foe. They did so in vast numbers and for a while set aside Irish internal conflicts with, perhaps, a sense of relief.

In World War II, into which Warnie was recalled, much the same pro-British 'neutrality' prevailed as Irish people, North and South flooded into the British Armed Forces and more than any other group in the Commonwealth distinguished themselves in the collecting of V.C.s and other decorations for gallantry. Important contact at the highest level was made between Irish and British comrades-in-arms. Indeed, at some of the most important 'Big Three' meetings half of Churchill's staff was Irish, while the list of great Commanders from Ireland was long: Alexander, Brooke, Cunningham, Dill, Montgomery among the best known. For most in Ireland there was no 'border' in the struggle against Hitler and, in what was known as 'aggressive neutrality' the Irish served the Allied cause at every level.

Tim Pat Coogan, the noted Dublin journalist and Editor, tells a whimsical story about the RAF which sums up this 'aggressive neutrality': 'The navigator of a wholly Irish bombing crew in a plane buffeted by flak over Berlin is said to have muttered under his breath over the intercom as something nasty came through the fuselage "Thank God de Valera kept us out of this".' (Timothy Patrick Coogan. Ireland Since the Rising (Pall Mall Press, 1966, p.89).

All of Ireland enjoyed the story and fully appreciated the special relationship which, regardless of politics, Ireland and Britain enjoy and exploit to their mutual benefit when the occasion requires. It makes for easier relations all around. C.S. Lewis was well aware of this and enjoyed to the full the camaraderie of his war service. In World War II he was not required for army service but he was delighted to be called upon to undertake an active lecturing Commission with the Royal Air Force. This experience gave him a permanent interest in the adult education movement and greatly improved his extra-mural contact.

By 1940 Lewis was quite at ease with the pattern of life that had evolved. He was earning his living and enjoying the experience at Oxford. But he never regarded being at Magdalen as 'being away from home'. Lewis drew an important distinction between Oxford and the nation state inside which it was placed - the University in his mind was in England but not part of England. This distinction is not as special as it sounds. After all, thousands of students since the foundation of Oxford University have made the journey to take lectures and tuition and then, because of the very short terms, returned to the base of their particular family or other social setting.

For Lewis it was a perfect arrangement - a bit like his later exclamation to me when visiting Parliament: 'All this and Heaven too!'. He had, indeed, the best of both worlds: his head was very much in Oxford but a large part of his heart was in Ulster and more particularly in Strandtown in the County Down. Through Arthur Greeves and the equally intimate Ewart link C.S. Lewis kept the channels of communication open; and with his great facility for adaptation he could at any time make a smooth transition from his intellectual workshop at Magdalen to his homeland in the County Down.

For a scholar who was to spend so much of his life in the cloisters of Oxford and Cambridge the Strandtown experience, based on the Ewart/Greeves social matrix, proved indispensable. It was a 'memory bank' which paid rich dividends and on which he was able to draw with pleasure and profit at every stage in his pilgrimage. Nor did he neglect his early endowments: instinctively, time and again, he returned to his Province to benefit from his investments and to enjoy the company of his trusted fellow shareholders.

Lewis thought much of these fellow shareholders and the village of Strandtown where they lived in full community; and this is where he found 'Joy'.

So, Strandtown lies at the heart of our quest for C.S. Lewis . Let us now explore it together.

CHAPTER SEVEN

Home and County Down Hinterland

At this stage in our Quest for Lewis we can be in no doubt about the significance of the Strandtown 'village' in his life. His love and longing for the place never faltered; though be enjoyed other settings there was a completeness in what his origins had to offer. Even in the last months of his life he was planning for Strandtown and other Irish outings. Who will ever forget his final crie de coeur to Arthur Greeves; or his constant insistence that it was in Strandtown that Warnie with his toy garden had made possible the unforgettable revelation of 'Joy', which ever after surfaced as one of life's singular events. As always, the complexity of Lewis has opened up a whole range for intellectual speculation about his discovery. However, this chapter on Strandtown represents a more down-to-earth attempt to penetrate the Strandtown experience, with the help of Lewis 'pointers'. It will also prepare the way to meet up with some of the institutions and their people making up the landscape of that village.

First a word about the beginnings of Strandtown and about its long history of separate development. Local historians have researched the area well and we have evidence of growth from Medieval times. There is an ecclesiastical history drawing on wider monastic activity centred on Holywood and other parts of the county Down. Reputedly there was a Holy Well in the neighbourhood which encouraged local pilgrimages but little growth in population. The cluster of people and cottages remained relatively unchanged for many centuries, occupying part of a long stretch of beach running from the nearby town of Belfast and known as the Long Strand - hence Strandtown. One of the early Big Houses was known by that name and occupied a prime site at Gelston's Corner in the centre of the village - an important gathering point then and now.

By 1700 Strandtown was a small country village straddling the road between the linen weavers village of Ballymacarrett, just outside old Belfast, and the better known village of Holywood, with its historic Church links and a priory founded in 1200AD. Holywood was part of the hinterland well known to Jack and Warnie as, on their bicycles, they explored their County Down. They would have noted parallel developments with Belfast as the 'new money' from industry and commence began to express itself in residential property developments in the early years of the Industrial Revolution which had come to the Lagan valley.

Already the wealthy merchants of Belfast had begun to build their stately homes in and around Holywood, Cunningham Greg at Ballymenoch, later owned by Sir Daniel Dixon, first Lord Mayor of Belfast, and Sir Samuel Kelly, coal merchant, near the site of the present Eventide Home. Redburn was another of these large houses, owned by the Dunville family, wine, tea and spirit merchants. Henry Murney, a Belfast tobacco merchant, built two large mansions at Tudor Park. All families with which the Lewises had personal or business links.

Holywood, like Strandtown, managed to absorb its newcomers and still retains many features of its more ancient past. But, being closer to Belfast the pace of change was quicker in Strandtown; and the surge of the Industrial Revolution, in which Belfast was to play such a significant role, changed the tenor of life in Strandtown as Big Houses with their attendant service support staff were erected throughout what was becoming a select and popular residential area.

As the industrialisation of Victorian Belfast pressed on, Strandtown was being described by local developers as 'a highly picturesque and healthy locality (important in fever conscious days) offering many sites for the erection of villa residences'. Or, as another put it in a press announcement in language well up to the standard of enthusiastic property developers of today, 'Strandtown offers many eligible sites for the erection of substantial villa residences in the neighbourhood of Belfast. It is, in all respects, one of the very best - affording at once delightful views of the bay, the town and the boldly diversified scenery of the Antrim Shore'. This scenic view the Lewis brothers were often to observe from their attic window in 'Little Lea'. They were enlivened by it.

So, Strandtown in the late 18th and early 19th Centuries was becoming a desirable place in which to live, for what was then the 'new rich', many of whom were to become the 'seriously rich' of Ulster. Strandtown would remain a village, but with a much more complicated infrastructure.

As in other Industrial Revolution towns, Belfast's Captains of Industry were anxious to leave their factories, shipyards and mills at night to refresh themselves in the surroundings of excellence which their new found wealth could afford. The advantages of the unspoilt beauty and non-polluted air of Strandtown was discovered and appreciated by the merchants who took to erecting splendid early Victorian residences, surrounded by ornate gardens. There was much interchange and considerable intermarriage between these powerful families. Their properties and estates were formidable in size, offering to those (like the Lewis brothers) who had family   connections, an opportunity to become part of an elaborate and influential 'Big House' social network stretching far and wide over Ireland and Britain. A local builder (born in 1906) told me that on the site of one such mansion, 'Ardvarna', which he acquired for development in the 1960s, he was able to erect fifty-seven substantial dwellings on the surrounding land. This gives some indication of the extent of the new estates which began to spring up in Strandtown and similar areas in the wake of the Industrial Revolution. Many of these estates were self-sufficient communities, offering a lifestyle which Lewis with his knowledge of Jane Austen's novels would have readily understood.

The list of newcomers to Strandtown in the 19th Century reads like a roll-call of the industrial great: Sir Wm. Quartus Ewart, world renowned flax spinner and linen manufacturer; Sir Otto Jaffe, German born, who did much to put Belfast on the map; another German, Gustav Wilhelm Wolff joined with Strandtown neighbour Sir Edward Harland to develop a world famous shipyard: Pirrie a man of many talents, Heyn in Shipping, Henderson in newspapers and McClure in building development. The list is long and impressive in its commercial and industrial influence. But these are only a few of the notables who flocked to the area after a day in the noise and smog of Belfast. In their relaxed setting they were a reminder of an historic Anglo - Irish description of neighbours: 'Close enough to excite curiosity, but far enough away to discourage intimacy.'

The people of Strandtown's Big Houses as I soon observed, were well known to Lewis and especially through the St. Mark's network. Many estates are still remembered in the area and when no longer in existence are perpetuated in the names of local streets: Harland Park, Wolff Street, Netherleigh, Helgor, Craigavon, Norwood, Schomberg, Glenmachan - they and many others recall the past. But, of course, for C.S. Lewis it was Glenmachan House that counted for most. As an early guide book recorded: 'Glenmachan House is the property of Sir William Ewart, a gentleman, originally of Scottish descent (one of many contributing to an historic 'mix'), well known for the liberality with which he supports all objects of public utility, and especially for his services on behalf of the Church of Ireland, since the untoward disendowment of that establishment'. Note here the unhappiness about the Disestablishment of the Church of Ireland which was still felt in young Jack Lewis' day. The Ewarts, of course, were powerful supporters of St. Mark's and subscribed generously to its development and upkeep.

The link is continued by Captain O.W.J. Henderson and his wife Primrose, daughter of Gundreda Forrest (née Ewart). Interestingly, Gundreda followed tradition and sent her daughter to Downe House in England. Downe House, founded in 1907 in Charles Darwin's home in Kent, aimed 'to provide girls with an holistic education that encourages them to strive for the highest academic results of which they are capable, while at the same time developing the personal, social, spiritual and emotional awareness that is the balance to academic excellence.'

While visiting recently with Canon Harvey and his wife Julien in Westminster Abbey I discovered that Mrs. Harvey, whose mother had links with Tolkien, attended Downe House at the same time as Mrs. Henderson. Such is the range of the Anglican network! Gundreda, of course, is immortalised for her beauty and personality in Lewis' writings and in a long life was closely associated with her birthplace.

When Glenmachan House came to be dismantled to make way for an impressive modern housing development there were many who mourned its passing. None more so than much respected local historian, Jim Patton, who was a witness to what for him was a solemn occasion. So much so that he salvaged a piece of the ornamental entrance arch which now has an honoured display place in his garden in Old Holywood Road.

Glenmachan lives on - such is the pull of history in Strandtown. It is good to see that freelance archaeologists are still around to preserve the past!

This short account of the Big Houses in Strandtown goes some way to indicate the power and pull they exerted in the social network of the time. They were central to Lewis in his formative years and throughout his life. No one discussing the experience with him, or reading Archbishop Caird's account of a social occasion with the Ewarts, could doubt the significance of the Big House link in the development of Lewis' character and his dedication to good works.

Of similar name, but a separate establishment (a Shillington House), Glenmachan Tower House is still in existence. In size, style and surroundings it gives some idea of Big House elegance. It brings back memories of an opulent and dignified past and Lewis spoke highly of the mansion and often stayed in it when it operated as an hotel.

For those of today who want to get the feel of former Big House glory Lewis would probably point to an old favourite of his, Bangor Castle. The Castle is now owned by the local Council and since 1994 much of it has been open to view by the public. It also houses a Heritage Centre and other amenities. Built in 1852 for Robert Edward Ward as a mansion house with its 155 acres of parkland, 35 bedrooms and extensive servant and stable yards, it represents life at the top in days gone by. Little did C.S. Lewis know on his early bicycle rides to the area that one day his Chaplain at Magdalene College, Cambridge, would be Simon Barrington-Ward, linked to the family of that name, well known in Victorian County Down.

But, of course, not all houses in Lewis' boyhood were big. Many were small and in Lewis school days belonged mainly to the servant class who worked for their wealthy employers. In one street near to Lewis' birthplace a Directory of the time gives a listing of gardeners, coachmen, cooks, butlers, rivetters, bricklayers and general labourers - and many other occupations associated with local needs. Many of these residents lived in nearby Wilgar Street and Dundela View and were well acquainted with Albert Lewis and his wife when they moved into Dundela Villas after their marriage in 1894. The Lewises joined the ranks of the local employers, taking on two servants and were regarded as good employers. The house which was rented to them by Thomas Keown, a relative, was no Big House, but it was by no means tiny. By the standards of the time it was a respectable first house for the newly weds and claims fame as the birthplace of Warnie and Jack. Unfortunately it is no longer in existence, but on the site of the Dundela Flats development a memorial plaque was erected in 1998 to mark the birthsite.

Of more enduring memory is the 10th Scout Hall (built in 1927) in nearby Oakland Avenue and built in the garden in which Warnie and Lewis often played. The Group had powerful backing from the local church and business establishment and became an important rallying point for the young people of Strandtown. It still retains considerable influence in Scouting locally and nationally and many local leaders have passed through its ranks. Lewis' cousin, Harry Keown, formed this famous Group of Baden Powell Scouts. Lewis always retained an affection for the Group and he is an honoured name among those in Strandtown with '10th' connections. The archives of the Group record the Lewis/Keown connection and give information about Dundela Villas, the first home of the Albert Lewis family. There is also an interesting picture collection of early days, many of which Lewis would recognise.

It is interesting to note that on the night that C.S. Lewis died we in the 10th Scout Group were having a special conference in the

Scout Hall and talking about times past when Lewis lived on the site. On that same evening we heard of President Kennedy's assassination.

They say that we always remember where we were when J.F.K. died. We in the '10th' have a twofold memory of that sad evening in 1963.

The house to which Albert Lewis brought Flora, his bride, was listed in the Belfast Census Return for 1901 as a '2nd Class Dwelling' with seven inhabited rooms (and five front windows) for a family of six persons (Albert, Florence, sons Warnie and Clive and two sevants). Also on the site were a stable, a coachhouse (the first headquarters of the 10th) and a harness room.

By Ewart standards Lewis' birthplace was a modest establishment; but it was also an emphatically comfortable and certainly happy middle-class home. However, Dundela Villas was but a stepping stone for Albert Lewis. A man of considerable legal and literary talents he was ambitious in both directions, all combined with political contributions in the Unionist cause of his time. He never liked the smoke and soot of industrial Belfast and like many of his contemporaries wanted to move more deeply into the leafy outskirts of Strandtown, preferably nearer to his highly regarded St. Mark's Church where his father-in-law was Rector. He was also aware that he had to 'do well' by his wife, marriage to whom 'had brought him up in the world' and whom he worshipped.

Hard work and careful planning smoothed the way and in 1905 the family moved to 'Little Lea', 76 Circular Road. He had had the home purpose-built for himself and family but never seemed satisfied with the structural outcome: he railed continually against what he considered poor standards of roofing and other building defects. But, as I have indicated earlier, local crafts-men, including my bricklayer father, never took his complaints all that seriously. Neither did Flora nor even the boys add much to his litany of imagined defects.

Interestingly, he never sought alternative accommodation. In fact he seemed content with 'Little Lea' and maintained it as a home base for the family for the rest of his days. It was also, of course, a prestigious address in a cluster of some of the most powerful people in Ireland. The area still attracts Ulster's 'top people'.

The house remains today a gracious private family home, maintained by Denis and Margaret Rogers. It is a spacious dwelling, and with its numerous reception rooms, bedrooms and multi-purpose areas 'Little Lea' must have seemed vast to Warnie and Jack - by any standard, it was quite sufficient to give them 'space' to ramble and to indulge their considerable powers of imagination. Equally, one can imagine the loneliness of the place for young Jack after he had lost his mother and when schooling arrangements all too often separated him from Warnie. But for a few years, with their mother as company, all was magic as they enjoyed the security of a happy and exciting home life. The boys with their attic study and an ample supply of books enjoyed each other's company and in writing and drawing expanded and stimulated shared imagination. From their attic windows there were commanding views of St.Mark's and other local landmarks - and not far away was the shipyard in which their Lewis relatives were often employed. They knew a great deal about 'the yard'. Indeed, years later, when they read in the Belfast Telegraph of 15 April, 1912 with its heading, 'Titanic Lost - an unparalleled shipping Calamity', it must have felt like the loss of an old friend, whose birth they had witnessed and whose progress they had followed along with local friends and relatives.

One other interesting 'Little Lea' attic feature is a small, child high' doorway leading into a cosy dormer area. It is very suggestive of a way-into a private world for children who might wish to explore together and beyond the range of adults. Looking at it, I wondered whether it might not serve as a 'Wardrobe' for those with imagination. Mrs. Rogers occasionally brings local children into this very special place at Christmas and other festive occasions. It is a pleasant link with a notable past. A plaque on the wall of 'Little Lea' reads- 'Ulster Historical Circle, C.S. Lewis (1898-1963) author and critic lived here, 1905-17.' My cousin, historian Victor Kelly, who helped to place it, was one of a small band of Lewisians who kept the work of Lewis alive locally in the lean years.

Happy days were spent by the Lewises in 'Little Lea' as they settled into what was a secure and enjoyable family life. Both Florence and Albert were well prepared by strength of character and upbringing for the task. Florence (Flora) Augusta Hamilton, whom Albert Lewis married in St. Mark's Dundela on 29 August, 1894, was the daughter of the Rev. Thomas Robert Hamilton, Rector of St. Mark's, whose family came from Queenstown, County Cork, and who had given distinguished service to the Anglican community in Rome before coming to Belfast. By all accounts Flora, though very young at the time, made good use of her time in Italy and from an early age gave indications of becoming an outstanding scholar. On settling down in St.Mark's Flora was prepared for entry to the local Queen's University where she proved a brilliant student of mathematics, passing with First Class Honours and gaining recognition as a leading student of her day, at a time when women were something of pioneers in higher education. Years later, C.S. Lewis gained a reputation among women students as a tutor who was ahead of his time in recognising their merits in the somewhat discouraging reception which they received at Oxford.

Albert Lewis , whose family was originally regarded as something of a 'blow-in' from Wales and County Cork, was himself sometimes suspected of having social pretentions. He very rapidly demonstrated his real worth and never more so than when his offer of marriage was accepted by the much admired Flora Hamilton. Still, Albert must have considered himself a very lucky man when he was ultimately accepted by Flora after she had turned down an offer by

HOLYWOOD ARCHES
by Thomas Clarke

The Strandtown Family

Father
Albert Lewis.

Grandfather Hamilton
of St. Mark's.

Jack's Mother, Florence
Lewis (known to the family
as Flora).

C. S. Lewis as a schoolboy.

Jack and Warnie - exploring Co. Down.

Warnie 1915 - home on leave.

Tennis Party at Glenmachan. Standing: Arthur Greeves, Gordon Ewart, Jack Lewis.

Young Jack with Ewart family group, 1913.

Gundreda Ewart - a favourite cousin.

Greeves Family Group - Arthur beside Lily, 1912.

Albert Lewis, Jack and Warnie - Glenmachan Garden Party, 1919.

C.S. Lewis - a study by Ross Wilson, 1998.

Helen Waddell - famous Ulster
Medieval scholar. Well known in
Lewis' Oxford.

George Heatherington (B. 1885) and Family - served in Big Houses - Ruby (centre) is an authority on Strandtown Village.

May Jamison and Annie Strahan - devoted housekeepers at Little Lea after 1908.

Dundela Villas - first home of Albert and Flora
Lewis - only known picture.
Painted by Alan Seaton.

Ty-Isa: Home of Grandfather Richard
Lewis. Picture (1998) includes Sir Ivan
Neill (friend of Arthur Greeves) who
acquired the property.

Bernagh - home of Arthur Greeves, opposite Little Lea.

Glenmachan 1902 - extended family home to Warnie and Jack.

Glenmachan Tower House. Another 'Big House' frequented by C.S.L.; especially
when it became a hotel.

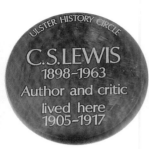

Little Lea.

Dundela Villas.

Forrest Reid home - Ormiston
Crescent, East Belfast.

Built in Dundela Villas' garden - founder
of the Group was cousin to Lewis.

Home of Forrest Reid - a literary rallying
point in East Belfast.

Favourite meeting place for Lewis and Greeves.

Strandtown Village - Meeting Points

Gelston's Corner, near Dundela Villas - local School and Church Hall supported by Ewart Family (1912).

Billy Graham's Barber Shop (1998).

Horatio Todd, Dr. Kenneth Bew, Ronnie Barr, Lily Newberry, Alan Seaton (friend of Ezra Pound).

Historic Chemist Shop fd. 1906 - important part of social network

St. Patrick's Newtownards Road by Thomas Clarke - Shipyard Streets of East Belfast,
well known to the Lewis family.

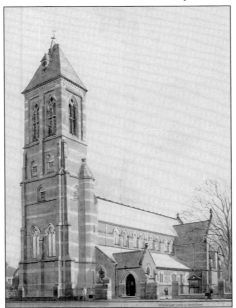

St. Mark's, Dundela by David Evans.

St. John Baptist Parish Church, Helen's Bay - a Lewis Church.

C. S. Lewis and Joy (and Arthur Greeves) were known here.

Linen Hall Library, Belfast, fd. 1788 - serving the whole community
since its inception.

Grand Opera House and next to the Hippodrome site - places where the
Lewis family relaxed.

Campbell College - with which Lewis had a brief encounter.

St. Anne's Cathedral, Belfast.

Father Walter Adams SSJE (1950) - C. S. Lewis' Spiritual Director.

SSJE Cloister, Oxford - Lewis' Monastery Garden.

SSJE Mission House, Oxford.

Friends, colleagues and former students of C. S. Lewis joined to share their memories of the man and his work at a unique gathering at Bangor Heritage Centre during the Aspects Festival. In attendance were, from left, Terence Brown, David Bleakley, Kenneth Irvine, Walter Hooper, Richard Murphy and Simon Barrington-Ward. September 1998: 'Spectator' Bangor.

his brother. Nor did she go out of her way to smooth Albert's path. She made it clear that friendship was at the heart of her feelings for him, but feelings strong enough to be going on with. The fact that Flora had also moved on to familiar first name terms was further reassurance to Albert and very wisely he decided to take the plunge - a decision which neither he nor Flora ever regretted as they built a happy home-life together.

Flora's many qualities extended to teaching and so young Jack from an early age had the privilege of receiving private tuition and was launched on a course of languages, reading, writing and arithmetic - studies which greatly encouraged the voracious hunger for knowledge which was discernible in the boy from his earliest days. His gift for words and memory were impressive and like a famous gifted boy from an earlier generation, John Stuart Mill, Jack Lewis had the capacity to surprise his elders with the precocity of his observations, which more than once pulled up adult conversationalists with a start, particularly where exactness of meaning was concerned. Even his father felt the weight of this disconcerting talent. Those who were his students at Oxford were aware of this facility, but to risk an encounter with it was a small price to pay for the privilege of conversation with its owner.

Flora was well able to handle her young charge and for the few years available her younger son flourished under her guidance and no doubt acquired the decided taste for private tuition which he never lost in subsequent years.

Even more pleasurable (but in the longer term counter-productive in terms of fatherly contact) were the holidays which the trio of Flora, Warnie and Jack took to taking together at home and overseas and to the exclusion of their father who was happier to stay at home to 'attend to business matters'.

This triangular relationship between mother and boys was in many ways eminently suitable and by all accounts it worked well, but, of course, when some years later Flora suddenly died everything went to pieces and neither the boys nor the father were able to find a substitute for the 'happy days with Mama', which the children remembered. A parting of the ways educationally and socially took place which added greatly to the trauma of mother-loss which they were to incur. Fortunately the Ewart family circle was at hand to offer amelioration for which their Lewis cousins were eternally grateful. So, from differing perspectives Albert, Warnie and Jack mourned deeply, (and throughout their lives) the early passing of a loving and gifted wife and mother.

Following the death of their mother in August, 1908, Jack and Warnie entered a very unsettled period emotionally and educationally. Warnie eventually found fulfilment in the Army; and Jack was rescued in 1914 by a meeting with William T. Kirkpatrick, an old friend of his father, who took him on as a private boarding student at his home in Great Bookham, Surrey. For each of the boys there was some sort of outlet for the grief they had endured in the years following their mother's death. Slowly they managed to adjust, though they still depended on and were protective of each other. Their father, they left very much to his own solutions, though the correspondence was maintained in domestic matters and moments of crisis. In later life they became more aware of their father's qualities and sacrifice, but in 1908 the old family certainties and solidarity were gone.

For Albert, though to the world he put on a good face, there was no relief. Thereafter, until his death in 1929, his inner life seemed to many to be one of quiet despair and a good deal of loneliness. Had he not lost his wife relatively early in their marriage - and through that death the companionship of his sons - there might have been a very different outcome; their marriage had all the potential of a powerful partnership. With 'Little Lea' as their base, and possessed of remarkable sons, they were well positioned to become a social catalyst in the setting in which Albert had very wisely chosen to base his family life.

One day the fuller story of Albert Lewis' life will be recorded, but even today there is a growing realisation that he has been considerably under-estimated, both as a father and a public servant. He was first generation middle-class and was fully aware of the implications of marrying into a family with an influential background. However, though from very different roots, he was part of a connection which had done well in an engineering world which was new and significant; many of its members were self-educated and gave much of their time to Church work and other good causes. The self-made artisan class in which Albert had originated was growing in confidence in a new industrial society which required its skills. Albert shared that confidence.

In the early days of his marriage Albert was very much 'the man about town' and was much in demand both as solicitor and as a speaker on literary or political occasions. The press of the time reported him regularly. He was also generous in his support for local good causes, particularly those to do with schemes for educational extension and local research initiatives. He thought highly of the Linen Hall Library and I note in a listing of the time that he is mentioned as one of the subscribers who made possible the publication of D. J. Owen's famous History of Belfast. In fact, his Belfast office in 83 Royal Avenue was very much a drop-in centre for the wide circle of friends and colleagues who shared his interests.

Fortunately Royal Avenue was centrally situated so Albert (and Jack and Warnie when they managed to be around) was well positioned to frequent the influential local political Clubs and to keep in touch with professional colleagues and public figures of the day with whom he was closely connected.

One other advantage of Royal Avenue was that Albert was in the close vicinity of the prestigious and historic Church centres of St.George and St. Ann and so was able to be involved in the day-to-day concerns of his beloved Church of Ireland. All of which won him considerable respect among his peers. C.S. Lewis, too, got to care for the local Churches - an affection which he shared with his sometimes estranged student, John Betjeman.

Albert was also held in high regard by those who worked for him at 'Little Lea' and it is a testimony to their satisfaction that there was little turnover in staff. He was generous with his professional advice and ran something in the nature of a 'free legal aid' scheme long before the system became public. The testimonies of the Great Knock and house servant Annie Strahan give evidence that this was so.

Perhaps a man is best known by his peers. In the obituaries which followed his death in 1929 some measure of Albert Lewis can be gleaned from the Belfast Telegraph, 26 September, 1929:

> *"The death of Mr. Lewis removes from our midst a strong upright man, a faithful friend, a keen and able advocate, a cultured and educated gentleman, and by his death the city in which his brilliant professional career was spent is appreciably the poorer.*
>
> *The news of his demise has been received with sincere sorrow by his professional colleagues, by the members of the judiciary and magistracy, and the officials of the various courts in the city, also by innumerable friends in civic and literary circles. The late Mr. Lewis was a broad-minded, tolerant gentleman, warm-hearted, kindly, and courteous, and his apparently reserved manner was the merest veneer to cover an essentially generous nature. In*

the legal world he was looked up to and admired for his deep knowledge and wide grasp; while he occupied a place in the affections of his colleagues which will be very hard to fill. His sympathies were all-embracing, and during the thirty- eight years he occupied the position of Police Court prosecuting solicitor for the Belfast Corporation he was universally recognised as a man of scrupulous fairness - one who, while determined to do his duty, never allowed his judgement to be warped by ill-feeling, but rigidly observed the dictates of humanity and charity.

The unostentatious aspects of the disposition of the late Mr. Lewis were to a certain extent known to his intimates, but he had an instinctive repugnance to allowing his acts to become known, and it might truly be said of him that he 'did good by stealth and blushed to find it fame'. A well-read and erudite man he found his chief recreation away from the atmosphere of courts of law in reading, and the classical and standard authors had in him a student of cultivated taste and deep appreciation. In the later years of his life he spent almost all his leisure time in this way, and especially did he find solace in books after the death of his beloved wife a number of years ago."

This snippet from a very extensive Obituary gives a picture of Albert Lewis as seen by those who worked with him. There is also a flavour of C.S.L. in the character description which brought out his extra-legal talents and his great love for Flora, his wife. A more humane and humorous side of Albert Lewis was appreciated by his contemporaries, but not always by his sons who seemed at times embarrassed by their story-telling father. As Lewis realised and made clear in later life he and Warnie were sometimes unfairly 'stuffy' about their father's often racy and characteristically Celtic sallies.

He could be droll, too. I give as a final tribute to Albert Lewis this story about his style in court:

THE LITTLE STONE-THROWER

Reference has been made to the humane spirit which Mr. Lewis displayed, in deserving cases, in the conduct of his prosecutions. An example may be quoted of an incident that occurred a number of years ago in the Children Court. A diminutive boy was charged by a burly constable with throwing stones at a chestnut tree, and Mr. Lewis elicited that there were no houses or windows in the vicinity, and that no passers-by had been endangered in the slightest. Addressing the Resident Magistrate, since deceased, he said sympathetically:

> *"I can't see that the little fellow has done any harm. He was only playing in a quiet place, and a few small stones wouldn't hurt the tree. The magistrate, however, took the attitude that 'there's too much of this sort of thing going on' and inflicted a fine of half-crown. "Well, well," said Mr. Lewis shaking his head as he sat down, "I only hope that when the Recording Angel comes to make up my account he will have nothing worse against me than throwing a few stones at a chestnut tree."*

I am sure that Jack and Warnie, who warmed to their father in his later years, would have enjoyed that example of their father in action.

CHAPTER EIGHT

Places and People of Strandtown

Our 'Overview' of Strandtown may have given the impression of a well ordered society into which everyone slotted neatly according to status. It was no such thing - in the 18th and 19th centuries it was becoming much more a socially over lapping sort-of-place with, however ill-defined, a growing recognition of interdependence. 'Ground Rules' there certainly were which separated social classes, but at the same time there was sufficient communal unity to produce that sense of belonging to the special village ambience which C.S. Lewis valued and publicised throughout his life.

As Lewis was always quick to point out, the best way to understand the community labyrinth into which he was born was to belong to it - to be a part of the charmed circle of Strandtown/Belmont folk who for him had a very special blend of kindness, intellect, fine judgement, immaculate taste and good looks. The list was praise unlimited and when I first came across it I was frankly amazed. Indeed, talking to Lewis one got the impression that he regarded his fellow villagers as almost a race apart, certainly superior or at least equal to any group be had ever come across. Most 'villagers' would not readily regard themselves as fitting the description. 'Absence makes the heart grow fonder' would be for them a more likely explanation of Lewis' enthusiasm. Lewis took the point, but did not regard it as invalidating his general thesis of Strandtown oneness.

Lewis was in no doubt, as any meeting with him for the first time made clear. He argued cogently that those born in the locality of Strandtown were part of a social network to which they were daily contributors and from which they could draw (as in his own case) comfort, confidence and a sense of belonging. Of course, the 'Big House' experience added powerfully to the sense of family which he enjoyed in Strandtown. Even a glance at early informal snapshots (and there are a great many) reveals the intimate and relaxed involvement with one another recorded by the camera during Ewart-Lewis-Greeves get togethers. There is certainly something substantial in the Lewis value judgement on Strandtown. Nowadays in our fast changing and ever more stereotyped society such networks as that to which he was drawn are increasingly difficult to find and preserve; though in the Irish setting there is clearer evidence than in England of continuity with the past and a desire to preserve one's roots. This aspect of Irishness was an essential element in Lewis' emotional makeup.

Within the Belfast of Lewis' day there were institutions which provided facilities for communal intermix: for young people, chief of these were the schools. There were many to choose from and this was especially true for well-off families. The Royal Belfast Academical Institution had long provided excellent education for the sons of Ulster's wealthy, including, for example, pioneer shipbuilder, Lord Pirrie; and the Methodist College had launched Flora, Jack's mother, on her spectacular academic career. Nearer at hand than any of these was Campbell College, a public school of renown providing boarding school facilities for the sons of leading businessmen, such as Sir William Ewart, John Andrews, Samuel Davidson and Sir Otto Jaffe. Arthur Greeves was also a pupil - what a pity that he and C.S.L. never met up with each other while at Campbell. But young Jack Lewis showed no enthusiasm for Campbell College during his six months enrolment. Later when he met so many of its former pupils (for example, Eric R. Dodds, Regius Professor of Greek at Oxford) at the top of their professions he may have regretted his acceptance (albeit initially reluctantly) of his father's decision to send him to England for boarding education. But whatever the reason for opting out of an Irish education (though his later studentship with 'The Great Knock' made up in some way for the separation), Lewis had to preserve his link with his native Province through institutions other than educational.

The Church was an obvious way in which to maintain such contact and for Lewis St. Mark's became a lifelong mainstay in keeping contact with his local roots. Perhaps it also prepared him for fellowship with the High Church Cowley Fathers into which he was to enter many years later, in 1930.

ST. MARK'S, DUNDELA

The origins of the Strandtown Church with which C.S. Lewis developed a lifelong association go back a long way. Although the parish of Dundela is a modern foundation, the name which it bears is an ancient one in the district. In a register compiled in 1302 Dundela is found as the name, apparently, of the ancient church of Knock, which for at least three centuries lay in ruins, adjoining the Knock graveyard. The name Dundela is believed to be derived from a prehistoric earthwork in the neighbourhood of the ruins.

Within the present parish of Dundela, in the grounds of the Moat House, there stood in old times the parish Church of Ballymeaghan, which belonged to the famous abbey of Bangor. Nothing now remains of this Church except the name, which survives in the townland of Ballymaghan, and a few sculptured tombstones.

In more modern times Strandtown formed part of the parish of Holywood, and before the Industrial Revolution it was a small village in a thinly populated countryside. In the middle of the 18th century, however, the population began to increase rather rapidly, and in order to meet the needs of the growing community a few local Church people arranged to have a Church service in the district on Sunday evenings. A coach-house in Sydenham park belonging to Mr. Henry Smith, was adapted for this purpose. The congregation soon found the coach-house Church too small for them, and their leaders then set to work to erect a new building at what is now Gelston's Corner, to serve as a school during the week and as a Church on Sundays. The Ewart family helped to run the Sunday School and some older residents of Strandtown still remember the occasions.

This early Church expansion scheme proved vital in the life of Strandtown and was particularly welcomed by the many who did not have means of transport and therefore found it difficult to reach either the parish Church in Holywood or that in Ballymacarrett. As local historian, J. C. Beckett, has observed:

'For the well-to- do, with their carriages, the distance was of little importance, but for the workers of Strandtown it meant a long walk'.

However, what was meant to meet a particular difficulty began to suggest greater possibilities; and so, a decade later, with the appointment of the far-seeing Thomas Robert Hamilton as Rector, a major Church extension plan was launched with the backing of an influential group of businessmen headed by outstanding Irish industrialist William Ewart, whose family has retained strong links with the Church since its foundation.

Perhaps surprisingly for Ireland the architect chosen was Englishman, William Butterfield (1814/1900) closely associated with the English Tractarian Movement. Probably the Ewart influence was at work here, believing in terms of excellence and ignoring the opposition which many in the Church of Ireland offered to 'the likes of Butterfield', as one critic put it. However, William Ewart had his way with the trustees and as the <u>History of St. Mark's Church Dundela, 1878-1978</u> puts it: 'One can only be thankful that the trustees were broadminded enough to employ the man who had designed both All Saint's, Margaret Street, London, and Keble College, Oxford, the two most popular rallying points of English High Churchmen.'

In consequence the Church of Ireland was given a Church (stone laid in 1876) of which they have been proud. As Sir John Betjeman (ironically, as we have already noted, not one of Lewis' favourite students!) an expert on such matters has affirmed, St. Mark's is 'Butterfield at his best'. The building process was drawn out for over twelve years. Then in 1891 the Ewart family, in a generous gift, in memory of Sir William Ewart, H.P., made possible the completion of the building. After a lapse of almost thirteen years Butterfield's original design was at last complete.

A recent Restoration Message from the Rector, the Revd. James Campbell, brings us up-to-date:

'We are privileged in St. Mark's to have inherited a beautiful and much-loved place of worship. It has most distinctive origins in that it is a Butterfield church and no

doubt helped to shape the young C.S. Lewis before he embarked on such a full and influential life. We wish to preserve our heritage, and to pass it on to generations to come. The people of St. Mark's are committed to that vision, and have given generously of their time, talents and money. But the task is an enormous one, and we seek the practical help of friends to complete it. Please support us in our determination to bequeath to those who follow a well-maintained Church dedicated to the glory of God.'

St. Mark's is important in the Lewis saga because at an early age it offered a natural centre of spiritual gravity from which he would always draw strength. He would drift from it from time to time, but as many of his insights indicate there is more than one way of arriving at our spiritual destination.

Though at times Lewis was out of sorts with worship in St. Mark's the Church of his parents remained an important 'way into' Strandtown and a means of affirming his identity. He was baptised there, he was confirmed there and it was in St. Mark's that he and Warnie placed their family memorials. Everywhere in St. Mark's the Lewis connection is evident: the font, the windows, the silver chalice. Then there is the front pew close to the pulpit. As archivist and historian Tony Wilson puts it: 'So the boy Jack would have been right under the eye of his grandfather while he was preaching the sermon.' And no doubt shifting uneasily when the great man was delivering one of his 'weepies'!

Today St. Mark's, 'Butterfield at his best, is a joy to visit - for those who want the fuller story Tony Wilson's Guide to the church is printed in our appendices.

With such an atmosphere surrounding his vital early days, the Irish saying resonates once again: 'Give me the child to seven and I will give you the man.' Lewis was being well prepared to face his 'dragons' on the spiritual trail. From time to time he ventured into alien territory, but always managed to return to home base.

Indeed in January 1963, a few months before his death, C.S. Lewis responded to an invitation to write an article for the new magazine of St. Mark's, <u>The Lion</u>. Robin Greer, Rector of Castlewellan, put me on the track of the script which, as Professor Beckett has remarked, 'may well become a collectors piece, for it includes a characteristic article contributed by C.S. Lewis, who had been born in the parish and spent his early days there.'

The then Rector, Edwin G. Parke, was delighted to have C.S. Lewis as a guest writer:

> *'We have been greatly encouraged by the fact that such a notable Christian author as C.S. Lewis has contributed to this present issue and we acknowledge his kind interest in the parish with which he had contact in his early days and where he still has ties of kinship.'*

I share the article in full as a reminder of how in days of considerable personal disruption and distress C.S. Lewis had time and thought to help the new magazine of his favourite parish get on its way.

THOUGHTS OF A CAMBRIDGE DON

This article was sent to us, at our request, by Dr. C.S. Lewis, Professor of English Literature at Magdalene College, Cambridge, to wish us well with our new magazine. The writer was once a boy in this parish, and is an Old Boy of Campbell College.

'Not long ago when I was using the collect of the Fourth Sunday after Trinity in my private prayers I found that I had made a slip of the tongue. I had meant to pray that I might so pass through things temporal that I finally lost not the things eternal; I found I had prayed so to pass through things eternal that I finally lost not the things temporal. Of course I don't think that slips of the tongue are sins. But I think some of them are significant, and I thought this was one of that sort. I thought that what I had inadvertently said very nearly expressed something I had really wished. Very nearly; not, of course, precisely!

Not too far!

I had never been stupid enough to think that the eternal could, strictly, be "passed" through". What I had wanted to pass through without prejudice to my things temporal was those hours or moments in which I attended to the eternal, in which I exposed myself to it!

I mean this sort of thing! I say my prayers, I read a book of devotion, I prepare for, or receive, the Sacrament. But while I do these things there is, so to speak, a voice inside me that urges caution. It tells me to be careful; to keep my head; not to go too far; not to burn my boats. I come into the presence of God with a great fear lest anything should happen to me within that presence which will prove too intolerably inconvenient when I have come out again into my 'ordinary life'.

I don't want to be carried away in to any resolution which I shall afterwards regret. For I know I shall be feeling quite different after breakfast; I don't want anything to happen to me at the Altar which will run up too big a bill to pay then. It would be very disagreeable, for instance, to take the duty of charity (while I am at the Altar) so seriously that, after breakfast, I had to tear up the really stunning reply I had written to an impudent correspondent yesterday and meant to post today. It would be very tiresome to commit myself to a programme of temperance which would cut off my after-breakfast cigarette.

A STORY FROM IRELAND!

The root principle of all these precautions is the same; to guard the things temporal. And I find some evidence that this temptation is not peculiar to me. A good author (whose name I have forgotten) asks somewhere, "Have we never risen from our knees in haste for fear God's will should become too unmistakable if we prayed longer?" An Irishwoman who had just been to Confession met on the steps of the chapel the other woman who was her greatest enemy in the village. The other woman let fly a torrent of abuse. "Isn't it a shame for ye," replied Biddy, "to be talking to me like that, ye coward, and me in a state of Grace the way I can't be answering ye? But you wait. I won't be in a state of Grace long!"

RECURRENT TEMPTATION

This is my recurrent temptation: to go down to that sea (I think St. John of the Cross calls God a Sea) and there neither dive nor swim nor float, but only dabble and splash, careful not to get out of my depth and holding on to the lifeline which connects with my things temporal. But that lifeline is really a deathline!'

This article by Lewis to his Irish church compatriots gives an interesting example of his ability to employ simple language in the service of profound thought, conveying a message which is common to all. How well, too, does Lewis warn us to see through ourselves; and to be prepared to discover that asking what is 'best' for us can sometimes be a perilous business. Little wonder that he often advised: 'Be careful, my friend, lest your prayers are answered!'

And then the happy language in his discussion about his Irish-woman's comment about her state of Grace. There is a humbling 'but for the Grace of God go I' suggestion in her final fling: 'But you wait. I won't be in a state of Grace long'! Interestingly, Lewis'

Irishwoman is described as standing on the steps of the 'Chapel' - here Lewis speaks in the language of his locality where to all concerned (and unlike England) Roman Catholics go to 'Chapel' and not 'Church').

C.S. Lewis shares a final thought: about the fear of plunging into the Sea which is God on to the lifeline of things temporal. His warning is clear - that lifeline is really a deathline!

Strong stuff for the Good Folk of St. Mark's - and, as Professor Beckett has observed, a bit of a collector's piece.

PRESBYTERIANISM

Though C.S. Lewis' early experience of church life was within the Church of Ireland setting of St. Mark's he could not but be also influenced by the Presbyterian tradition which was strong in Strandtown as elsewhere in Ulster. Indeed as local Presbyterian historian, Noel Nesbitt, has recorded, Presbyterianism in Strandtown predates the Church of Ireland; and from the 1840s missionary activity in the village was carried on by leaders from the nearby Ballymacarrett Presbyterian Church. Prominent businessmen took the matter further, and by 1862 the annual report of the local Belmont Presbyterian Church records an encouraging attendance of 239 and a total income of £414. Since then Presbyterianism in Strandtown has had a formidable following attracting the loyalty of some of Ulster's most notable citizens: Lord Pirrie the shipping Magnate, J.A. Henderson proprietor of the **Belfast NewsLetter**, and Lord Craigavon to name but a few. So, like St. Mark's, the local Presbyterian church could call on the great and the good of the time for support. By any standard it was a pivotal force in the life of the district and at the very least its members could claim parity of esteem with their Anglican neighbours.

Nor was the Church of Ireland a majority church. As census figures for the time showed, the Church of Ireland was the Church of only a minority and in fact amounted to about one-eighth of the total Irish population, and even in Belfast they were less numerous than either the Presbyterians or the Roman Catholics. Disestablishment also meant that Lewis' parents belonged to the first Church of Ireland generation who had to depend solely on their own efforts for the maintenance of parochial life.

Thus, Lewis was born into an Ulster society where Church of Ireland and Presbyterians found it advantageous to cooperate with one another on great issues of the day. His father was deeply involved in such initiatives-perhaps, as a result, some early intimations of the value of ecumenism may have 'rubbed off' on his young son. It is interesting to note, for instance, that in 1941 when the BBC was searching for 'a layman to address the nation on religious matters' the invitation came to Lewis from Eric Fenn, an eminent Presbyterian in the employ of the Corporation at that time.

No doubt Lewis' varied Ulster experiences (Greeves provided yet another dimension) stood him in good stead with Fenn. Certainly Lewis can never be accused of being narrow minded in his presentation of the Gospel truths. His popular pronouncements in broadcasting and journalism testify to his Christian outreach.

At an impressionable age C.S.L. was being exposed to an interchurch ethos calling for co-operation between Presbyterian and Church of Ireland members. Theological differences were often set aside when historic issues were at stake. Lewis' father was deeply involved in such discussions and the boys during school holidays were often reminded of the local tensions centred on the Craigavon estate close to 'Little Lea'. C.S. Lewis remained pro-Union in debates about Empire, but he never 'signed up' for any of the contending parties and throughout his life was even-handed with political groups in Britain. Certainly, those of us who were students had nothing to complain about on that score. The impression remains that his Strandtown experience contributed to the down-to-earth ecumenism which was to be a central part of his Christian witness in later years.

JACK AND WARNIE - EXPLORING STRANDTOWN TOGETHER

Jack and Warnie (young Jack often took the initiative) were great ones for exploring and Strandtown had much to offer. As they soon discovered, 'every village has its rallying points - places where everyday business is conducted, yet, at the same time, allows time for discussions with a wider range of shared concern. It has much to do with 'small being beautiful' - human cluster points which provide space for the ordinary things which give meaning to life. Lewis was to spend a lifetime digging out such 'things'.

Social rallying points are often most effective when they develop around a long-standing local figure with a reputation for being 'a good person to go to for a piece of advice'. Altogether someone who can be trusted - far enough away from the responsibilities of office to be independent, but close enough to wield considerable influence.

There were many such as these in Lewis' Strandtown. Gelstons Corner (near first home Dundela Villas) was a popular area to explore. Balmer's, for instance, on its prime corner site (still well preserved) had a great range of popular household goods and medicines to offer and a proprietor who knew the difference between the 'price' of things and the 'value' factor. The shop has continued as a link in Strandtown's 'humanity' chain by becoming a well supported dental centre. The building, with strong Lewis associations, offers service by popular local dentist James B. McIlroy, who often passes on news of Lewis. A pleasant bonus is to sit in the treatment chair and at the same time admire the across-the-street view of the site of the famous Strandtown National School and Church planted by St. Mark's, both closely associated with the Ewart and Lewis families. In this dental setting, with such literary associations, the 'between fillings' conversation can be excellent!

Further down the Holywood Road towards the equally famous Arches stood the barber's shop pioneered by a local group of Victorian hairdressers and associated with the name of Billy Graham known to generations from the village. Today, run by Billy's early 'soap' boy, Billy Walsh, who carries on the tradition, the business is now one of forty-seven hairdressers in the square mile, whereas early in the century it was one of only two. This latter point was important because it ensured a gathering-together of all who needed barbering attention and was a significant meeting point for the Lewis family and all others who chose to use it. C.S. Lewis knew of the shop and more especially did father Albert who lived just round the corner in Parkgate Avenue's "Ty-Isa".

Many famous establishment figures, and others less well known, have sat on the benches awaiting their turn. Those who know their Belfast will recognise writers like Sam Thompson, John Hewitt, Sam Hanna Bell, Forrest Reid and public figures like Lord Glentoran, Sir Ivan Neill, Harry Midgley, Ian Paisley and Tom Boyd.

Billy Graham, who was one of the district's pioneer barbers, was a well known local figure and benefactor. He also helped out with swimming courses at Campbell College and with hairdressing (again the communal overlap) and knew many of its staff and pupils. More demonstratively Billy Graham was a foremost radical who espoused the Labour cause and, indeed, once provided the election deposit of £150 (big money in those days) which helped to elect the first Labour M.P. for the district. His shop was regarded as something of an outpost for reform and was much approved of by the local trade union movement. But in practice most of his customers in search of a good haircut worried little about such additions to the service! However, the socialising influence of such institutions was important in early Strandtown.

Of much more practical significance to the Lewis boys in their explorations was the discovery and use of the local bicycle shop to which regular visits had to be paid to keep their machines in order. They were protective of their machines and were ever anxious to keep them in good repair. As the boys put it so often, when young and older: 'We have thumbs for nothing'. Such was a great affliction when trying to fix the link of a bicycle chain or to undertake brake repairs. Throughout his cycling life Lewis required help with such maintenance and in his Strandtown days visits to the local bike shop were essential. An important socialising bonus of such visits was the opportunity to get to know the young locals who gathered around cycling shops to compare models and to keep up to date with the considerable Irish love affair (then as now) with the much promoted new machine, simple to operate and requiring only pedal power to fuel it. For C.S. Lewis the bicycle was a key factor in his social life and a great enabler in Strandtown hinterland explorations. Jimmy Reid, who perpetuated an earlier tradition of local bicycle mechanics, was a popular figure in Strandtown. He provided an important neighbourhood service and gave his young customers an opportunity to mix with one another in an informal club atmosphere revolving around a common interest in their prized possessions.

HORATIO TODD'S - MORE THAN A CHEMIST'S SHOP

By far the most important of the informal gathering points in Strandtown at the turn of the 20th century was Horatio Todd's Chemist Shop at 72 Holywood Road, near the Arches. It was founded in 1906 and still exists.

Horatio Todd (named after Nelson and the shop was called 'Trafalgar') was born in 1878 and died in 1973. He had a long and active life as a chemist and prominent public figure - in both spheres he became President, first for the Pharmaceutical Society of Northern Ireland and then for the East Belfast Imperial Unionist Association. In Church matters he was closely identified with Belmont Presbyterian Church. His political activity brought him into regular contact with Albert Lewis who for many years had lived in the nearby family home of "Ty-Isa". With such connections Todd's outreach was considerable.

The 'Big Houses' and most of the artisan class used Todd's as their dispensary. His premises became a centre where one was likely to encounter an influential cross-section of the local community and business was likely to range beyond the purely medical. However, Todd never neglected his professional duties. He was famous for his personal prescriptions and for many his popular remedies seemed far ahead of traditional medical advice. He even kept contact with Buckingham Palace and from time to time the Queen received his products including at Christmas a collection of his special creation of Ulster Perfumes. Animals, too, were catered for and his large collection of tropical birds was on display from time to time. A man of many talents, he dressed the part in formal Victorian splendour. Little wonder that children flocked with their parents to the 'Trafalgar'. The Lewis family was well known in the shop.

For those with literary inclinations Todd's was something of a magnet -St. John Ervine, Forrest Reid, and, of course, Lewis and Greeves were among the callers. A more commented upon literary contact was with Estan Litvinoff, refugee niece of the Russian Foreign Minister who had become domiciled in Belfast and lived close to Todd's shop. Older inhabitants of Strandtown remember this interesting woman who helped many local artists. Stanley Spenser, the painter, owes much to her patronage.

But a famous 'Trafalgar' incident, which no doubt appealed to Lewis, concerned Ezra Pound. The American poet had been interned in Italy following World War II, when he had been accused of un-American activity. Todd's became involved when staff chemist Alan Seaton (himself a painter and writer) stepped in by writing to Pound offering sympathy and assistance. The poet replied with grateful thanks and asked Seaton to 'be my oxygen supply of information'.

The news leaked out and the Americans were not amused. Locals still talk about the day the

> *'Special Agents from Washington' turned up at Todd's to investigate the goings-on between Seaton and Pound. A correspondence (which has been preserved for posterity) followed, and eventually the crisis blew over, Seaton escaping with a caution. However, Pound never forgot the gesture of a stranger from Belfast. Some years later he invited his Irish friend to meet him in America where the reinstated Ezra Pound expressed his gratitude to Alan Seaton for concern 'which offered a lifeline when most needed.'*

It says much for Todd's liberality of mind that he took such an episode in his stride in the immediate post-war world when Pound was a figure of considerable controversy and when national nerves were raw.

Such incidents, and there were many others, give some idea of the vitality which surfaced day by day in the seemingly tranquil village of Strandtown. It was for C.S. Lewis a place where things really happened.

Voices from Strandtown

I have realised for some time that many of us in Ireland belong to a 'silent University' of men and women who are students of 'things Lewis' without being aware that there are many around us who are members of the same Lewis 'faculty' , studying a common curriculum.

Such is the case of our first contributor Ivan Neill (later, 1973, Sir Ivan) who, along with his wife Lady Margaret, lived close to Little Lea and was a friend and companion of Arthur Greeves from across-the-road Bernagh. My wife and I, from a younger generation,have known the Neill's for a lifetime and at one time lived close to them in the shipyard area of East Belfast. Later our paths met up in the Northern Ireland Parliament where Ivan had a distinguished Cabinet career, ending up as last Speaker of the House of Commons. He served as an officer in the Royal Engineers during the War and was a leading participant in the building industry of East Belfast. His various public activities, combined with active church membership made him very much a part of the local network of shared interests.

When we discovered our common interest in Lewis we had much to discuss - I with my Oxford experience and he with his close friendship with Arthur Greeves. Greeves, whom I knew only at a distance, deeply appreciated the company which the Neill family circle offered. During the War years he helped Margaret Neill with local voluntary services and especially in organising the weekly meetings of the Officer's Christian Circle which she organised in her Circular Road home. A recent letter from Sir Ivan helps fill in the details:

> *'My wife and I took up residence at Circular Road, Belfast in 1938. It was then a sparsely populated neighbourhood, bordering on what was regarded as a spread-out group of imposing residences, occupied mainly by families who had prospered in the then flourishing linen industry.*
>
> *One of the families, the Ewart' s,was related by marriage to C.S. Lewis . The social contacts were an important factor in the lives of this closely integrated community. In their early days Arthur Greeves and C .S.Lewis had frequent contact with these families and must have been influenced by their life style. Greeves and Lewis lived on opposite sides of Circular Road; Lewis in Little Lea and Greeves in Bernagh,later to be renamed Red Hall. Our home was in close proximity to Greeves and Lewis. '*

Sir Ivan continues:

> *'Soon after we took up residence at Circular Road,we were in contact and made friends with Arthur Greeves. C.S. Lewis had gone to Oxford and it was not our pleasure to make acquaintance with him. Greeves was a tall*

sparsely built man, not an imposing character. He lived with his brother John at Bernagh. John was involved in the family business of J. and T.M.Greeves,a large linen firm employing many workers in West Belfast. John was a cold hard man in contrast to the finer character of Arthur.

They had little in common and lived almost separate lives. Arthur was a complex character, intelligent and,gifted as a painter, but lacking in self confidence. We gradually won his confidence and he often sought my wife's advice about his problems, without ever imparting his close personal feelings. Arthur was an example of how much can be missed in life,when self-confidence is absent. It was this weakness in his character that made him depend so much on C.S. Lewis ,when a confidence developed in their early years.

In the early years of the 1939-45 war he joined in our involvement with air raid patrols,and showed himself a man not without a sense of duty. I was commissioned in the Royal Engineers in 1941 and stationed at Victoria Barracks,Belfast where I had been serving in a civilian capacity and soon became involved in the activities of the Officer's Christian Union. We organised a social evening at our home,and entertained a group of men and women from the three Services each Friday evening. There was a constant change of persons as postings followed one upon another. Arthur Greeves joined with a few of our other friends to help us entertain our visiting serviceman and women. It was in this atmosphere that we saw him relax and enjoy social contacts.

When I was posted overseas,my wife,with the help of Greeves and our other friends carried on the meeting until the end of the war.

I renewed my friendship with Arthur when I returned from service overseas. I entered public life in 1946, becoming a Member of the Belfast City Council, and later became M.P. for Ballynafeigh, in South Belfast. I now led a busy life and saw less of Arthur, who had no love for politics. Our meetings were now less frequent.

In the summer of 1954 we were away for three months on a goodwill tour of U.S. and Canada and our home was closed. Soon after our return Arthur moved from Bernagh to a house, Silver Hill, at Crawfordsburn. We maintained our friendship until his death.

Yours,
Ivan Neill,
May, 1998.

This letter from Sir Ivan Neill gives an insight into the non-literary Arthur Greeves – how he must have missed the reassuring presence of his Diary soulmate. But the connection with the Neill family was important: it provided a secure base for Arthur and one where he always felt useful. Many happy painting and walking holidays were spent together - the Rosapenna Hotel at Downings, Co. Donegal was a favourite venue. But even in those splendid surrounding Arthur complained that the beds were too short for his considerable proportions! As a painter he was also touchy about the weather regarding the slightest wind as a 'great gale making painting impossible.' But Arthur was always regarded as good company. When got going he could be a good talker. He was also happy on the piano and, more shyly, a keen amateur magician.

For my own part I got the impression of a polite, very shy man, with considerable talent linked to diffidence. We occasionally passed 'the time of day', but discussions would be general and never did he discuss his friend Jack. At times he could be waggish, though many regarded him as withdrawn. However, his letters with Lewis are more than enough to win him an honoured place in the literature of our time.

P.S. - an interesting footnote to Sir Ivan Neill the builder: when 'Ty-Isa' left the ownership of the Lewis family it was eventually purchased by Ivan Neill so that its surrounding ground might be made available for a new housing estate. Fortunately the house was allowed to remain. It is still occupied and well cared for; but, isolated as it is it lives up to its Welsh name which, roughly trans- lated , means 'the home alone'. I often thank my friend for sparing it for posterity !

Our next contributor is from Strandtown fellow-villager, James Nelson. James is a prominent local businessman with whom I transacted insurance matters for many years before we discovered our common literary interest. Rather in the way that Lewis and Greeves experienced a 'Do you like that' encounter on **Myths of the Norsemen** , so it was with James and me.

It happened on a business visit one morning when I left on his desk a Lewis book edited by our mutual friend Walter Hooper. Immediately we got things into perspective: we both enjoyed C.S. Lewis. Financial matters were set aside as we shared views on our hero.

James Nelson tells his own story and at the same time indicates a good deal of the common ground on which Lewisians of East Belfast meet:-

FROM: J.A. NELSON, SCHOMBERG PARK , BELFAST.
PERSONAL REMINISCENCES OF C.S. LEWIS

I well remember as a teenager hearing the first live
Broadcasts of C.S. Lewis. I did not know at that time that

the broadcaster was not only an Ulsterman but a Belfastman and an East Belfastman at that. Born and bred near the Holywood Arches, I lived in the same district as this Christian teacher, so soon to become world-famous for lucid writings and expositions. I realised that he had lived for many years within a mile of where I was born and even now I still live within a mile of his home at 'Little Lea'. As I go to visit my grandchildren who live about two miles on the other side of the Lewis home I can pass his house but often I divert up the Holywood Hills over which he loved to ramble as a boy. He enjoyed the beautiful views over Belfast Lough and in the distance he could see Slemish Mountain where that earlier great Christian, St. Patrick, roamed in his young days.

A few years ago I listened to a distinguished preacher in a local church and I was struck by the clearly reasoned nature of his address. Afterwards I asked him if he was a devotee of C.S. Lewis, tho' no reference was made; he agreed he was and accepted the compliment. Another preacher referred to C.S.L. and on speaking to him he told me that Douglas Gresham, the stepson was a member of the congregation of which he is the Minister. I called at the church in Kilkenny but unfortunately neither Douglas nor the Minister was there.

I remember David Bleakley, the local Member of Parliament, calling at my place of business and how delighted I was to know that he was also an enthusiastic admirer of the Lewis writings and indeed had actually known the great man.

My father-in-law was a Director of the local Greeves Firm with whose family C.S. Lewis had such close links.

As a young Christian I enjoyed his works so much; never was it easy to completely follow that agile mind and with increasing years I do not always find it much easier. But here is a man of whom East Belfast has a right to be proud and he in turn was proud to be an East Belfastman.

(sgd) James A. Nelson,
10th June, 1998.

Equally significant is the impact which Lewis made on more recent villagers. An outstanding example is Dr. John Gillespie, from working class East Belfast. John, Senior Lecturer at the University of Ulster and a noted Lewis scholar, shares the excitement of discovering C. S. Lewis as 'a Godsend.'

LETTER FROM JOHN GILLESPIE, GROWING UP WITH C. S. LEWIS

I first got to know about C. S. Lewis through reading **The Screwtape Letters** *when I was in Upper Sixth, captivated by the wit and originality of Screwtape's demonic advice to his soon-to-be-devoured nephew Wormwood. Screwtape's attempts to trick Christians into leaving the straight and narrow showed Lewis' rare insight into our spiritual behaviour. The effect was all the greater when I discovered that Lewis came from the same part of East Belfast as I did (I lived about half a mile from the site of Dundela Villas) and that he had been a successful academic at Oxford and Cambridge. Coming from a Christian family from which no-one had gone to University, this made a tremendous impression on me.*

At RBAI, a leading Belfast school, and from the following year at Queen's University, I was aware of the prevailing view that intelligent people did not believe in Christianity and its myths, although they could safely admire Christ's moral teaching.

*So C. S. Lewis was a Godsend to me, for he showed me that orthodox Christianity was neither irrational nor incredible. Since then I have been growing up with Lewis, both intellectually and spiritually. In my early days at University I struggle with many doubts - about God's existence, the problem of evil and so on. As a student of modern English, French and German literature I came up against many opponents of Christianity such as the existentialist Jean-Paul Sartre and the humanist Albert Camus. Although others were helpful to me, the role of C. S. Lewis was critical. I moved on from Screwtape to works of apologetics such as **The Problem of Pain**, and **Miracles** and, most significantly of all, the auto-biographical **Surprised by Joy**. Here was someone from the same part of the world as I was, steeped, like me, in the Northernness of Irish skies, with an understanding and longing for something beyond (characterised as joy), yet someone who had been through much deeper waters than I was experiencing. The story of how Lewis lost his faith, found his way back to God by seeing the intellectual inadequacy of atheism and ultimately turned to Christ was significant in underpinning my own faith. And the vivid clarity of **Mere Christianity** helped me understand its key elements. So the arguments against Christianity were not overwhelming after all - indeed the opposite is true.*

*Lewis, then, was most important to me at this stage as a defender of the faith. Going on to doctrinal research (into anti-Christian writers) and then academic life, this debt increased as a I read more, including the marvellous Narnia tales. I have continued to read (and reread) his works - his sermons, essays, imaginative writing, letters and literary criticism - and they are still helpful and challenging. The key text for me has been **The Abolition of Man**, whose insights into natural and moral law were so crucial for my work at one stage that I read it four times in three months. I have often turned to it since. Then there is his inaugural lecture at Cambridge, 'De Descriptione Temporum', with its masterly overview of modern culture.*

What is striking is the breadth and integrity of Lewis' thought. He presents a clear, consistent, unified view of Christianity, and outlines its most important truths, defending them vigorously, without a trace of sectarianism, and with a great understanding of the heart of man. He has been a tremendous example for me both in his courage in taking the unpopular road of standing for Christian truth in academic life and in his capacity to communicate so readably, to all kinds of people all over the world, without a hint of jargon.

*However his most significant contribution has not merely been to explain and defend the moral and intellectual truth of Christianity, but to make the spiritual come alive in his writings, such as in his depiction of the Oyarsa in **Out of the Silent Planet** or the death of Old Narnia, the ascent from the Shadowlands at the end of **The Last Battle.** He shows the glory of God and the good, as well as the horror and reality of the struggle with evil, as* *exemplified in Ransom's combat with Weston/the Unman in **Voyage to Venus**. This is a feat that few writers have matched this century.*

John Gillespie,
October 23, 1998

These three 'Strandtown Voices' provide clues to Lewis as a writer, but there are still those who provide information about his boyhood, giving substance to the saying: 'Give me the child to the age of seven and I will give you the man.'

I began my information gathering among those who had served in the Lewis /Greeves Ewart households and in particular with those in their '80s and 90s who had been family retainers.

My first witnesses came from the well known Heatherington family of seven who lived in Dundela View, a small street of working class homes (still there) overlooking and a few minutes away from the Lewis birthplace in Dundela Villas. This family was headed by George Heatherington (1885-1945) who was for some time the Lewis milkman. Later, when he qualified as a Master Builder, he was available for maintenance work on Little Lea. George was a great source of information about 'goings on' at the Lewis home and spoke affectionately of the family and especially Albert who was always dubbed by him 'Lewis of Little Lea'. Lewis' mother was for him 'a real lady, very well read who always brightened your day.' He was a great source of information to those of us from a younger generation.

The Heatherington circle also provided domestic help and daughter Ruby (Christened in St.Marks, Dundela) remembers life in the Big Houses when she accompanied her aunt on her daily service visits, particularly to Schomberg and other popular venues for Jack and Warnie.

Ruby remembers Schomberg for its elegance and size: 'I'd never seen as big a place. The fireplace seemed big enough to burn the trunk of a tree and the bed-rooms were vast, making it possible for the bed to be in the middle of the room with space to walk round it - all with yards to spare.'

Ruby Heatherington (now Purdy) provides yet another link with the Lewis connection. She, with her brothers, attended the local Sunday School run by Gordon Ewart in Strandtown; it catered for the working class children of the district. She was also a visitor to Richard Lewis' house 'Ty-Isa' in the 1920's when with her sister she shopped at the market garden established in the extensive gardens of 'Ty-Isa' by its enterprising owner. Along with the children of the area she enjoyed the swingboat which Richard Lewis had constructed as a recreation point for the children of customers. Later in life Ruby, with her husband David Purdy, helped to form the influential East Belfast Historical Society which has encouraged local social history studies, many of which she has recorded for BBC Northern Ireland.

More direct contact with the Lewis family at 'Little Lea' came through servants Annie Strahan and May Jamison who were taken on as live-in helps after the death of Albert Lewis' wife in 1908. Annie Strahan (later Mrs.McCrea) left 'Little Lea' in 1917 to get married (in St.Mark's), but kept contact with the house until Albert Lewis died in 1929. He welcomed her visits. Annie died in 1972, but her son Victor has many memories of 'Little Lea' retailed through his mother.

Victor remembers Albert Lewis a 'a kindly smiling-faced man who always gave a welcome' - even when Annie arrived on the doorstep with her brood of five children! Albert, no doubt lonely because of Jack's regular spells of absence, seemed glad to receive such visits and Victor has happy memories of the generous gifts ('sometimes as much as a half crown !') bestowed by Albert Lewis on such occasions. Annie Strahan stories of 'Little Lea' were happy ones; and with an annual wage of £20, plus full board and lodgings and good holidays, she considered herself well treated.

The Lewis boys were remembered as 'an inseparable pair' who sorely missed their mother and 'who should not have been sent off to England so soon after her death.' They were 'as bright as buttons, though young Master Jack often took the lead.'

According to Victor, Jack and Warnie called their father 'Papy', so 'my mother always talked about 'Papy Lewis.' One story which Annie passed on has to do with night noises:-

> *'I remember her saying she and Mary could hear a tapping noise late at night when they were relaxing in their room and they wondered if the place was haunted. They found out later that it was 'Papy' knocking out his pipe on the hearth before be retired for the night.'*

Victor also passes on two delightful stories about Jack and Warnie related by his mother.

On one occasion she prepared a 'posh meal', as she described it, for the boys and told them to 'eat it up' while she was out. Annie returned sooner than expected and found the boys engaged in a mock funeral service in the garden. A hole had been dug and the unacceptable 'posh' dinner was being quietly buried! Annie interrupted the ceremony just as the boys were solemnly parading around the remains, chanting the Dead March from Saul as their mark of respect!

One other amusing culinary occasion related by Annie to her son goes thus: 'We were sitting at dinner one day when I saw Warnie peering hard into the silver lid of the soup tureen. Turning to Jack he asked: 'Why is it, Jack, that when I look at my reflection in the silver lid of this tureen my features are distorted?' Jack replied: 'Dear Warnie, why do you assume that your features <u>are</u> distorted - maybe that's the way you really look.' Precocious children, indeed!

Stories such as this give something of the day to day flavour of what went on in the Lewis and other houses of top people at the turn of the Century.

But not all of our information comes from the distaff side - male servants, also had a close affinity with their employers in their everyday problems. This was particularly so once the motor car began to assert its ascendancy over horsedrawn vehicles. Arthur Power (B.1910) of East Belfast's engineering fraternity, and part of a well connected 'good with motor cars' family, assured me that the Ewart/Greeves/Lewis circle were 'sold on motor cars' at an early stage. Living in a city which boasted many outstanding inventors like John Dunlop, whose invention of the pneumatic tyre made possible the success of the motor car, it was to be expected that enthusiasm for the vehicle among leading citizens would be strong.

But as Arthur Power and his fellow artisans often observed 'the gentry may buy their expensive cars, but they need people like us to keep them going - and sometime to even get them started!'

Young Jack Lewis was no exception and his conversation and letters often allude to the rôle of the car in family life. For instance, writing to his favourite cousin Gundreda he engaged in a discussion about the merits of a streamlined car as opposed to a beautifully run house. Cars were often on the conversation agenda and especially the merit of Ford versus Rolls Royce. Indeed on one occasion Kelsie Ewart greatly annoyed cousin Jack when she gave the impression of being snobbish about the ownership of a family Rolls, fearing that they might not become 'too popular'.

However, notwithstanding the impression given in the film 'Shadowlands', Lewis never learned to drive and was fortunate in being able to depend on the help of Arthur Greeves and other friends. I often wondered why this was so and assumed it could be put down to his fatalism about 'being useless' at hand skills. As he despaired: 'You engineers have hands for anything; I have thumbs for nothing but writing.' Fortunate for Lewis lovers!

Of course, he also grew up in a world where public transport was being steadily improved. It was readily available and very comfortable, especially for those able to pay for comfort. He was always supportive of public transport and indeed probably looked forward to a trip on the Titanic in which he had Belfast pride and on the ill fate of which his correspondence made comment.

These testimonies from those who provided the social fabric for Lewis and his family circle indicate that he was fully at home with his local upbringing and was being well prepared for the social setting of the Oxford which he was one day to enter. He fitted into that Oxford just as readily as he fitted into his Strandtown village and the surrounding County Down on his return at any time. As generations of Oxford graduates will confirm, there was nothing unusual in this ability to adapt, especially for those who had a welcoming and stimulating home base.

AN ARCHBISHOP REMEMBERS

How well C.S. Lewis fitted into his place of birth is splendidly illustrated in a very personal letter from Archbishop Donald Caird, Honorary Archbishop of Dublin, a lifelong admirer of Lewis.

Donald Caird's letter is a warm and grateful account of a social occasion with C.S.L. I quote it at length because of the way it brings out the full flavour of our subject. It also tells much about links with the Ewart family. Above all it emphasises the generosity of Lewis' social outreach and his capacity to leave an enduring memory with those who met him.

Archbishop Caird's letter goes thus:

'When I was a Curate in St. Mark's, Dundela, 1950-54, C.S. Lewis used to visit the Ewart family at Glenmachan. They were his cousins:

Miss Kelsie Ewart on occasion invited me to dinner, probably 1951 or 1952. I was greatly thrilled to meet the man whose books enthralled me and whose presentation and defence of Christianity to my generation I regarded as superb.

I was not in the least disappointed in meeting my hero in the flesh. In appearance he was a much bigger man than I had anticipated. He looked, I thought, more like a County Down farmer than a very distinguished Oxford academic. He was tall, well built, with black hair brushed back from his forehead. He had a broad open face which relaxed into a charming smile, and a beautiful deep speaking voice which he used to great effect in conversation.

"His great delight", he said, "was to walk in the County Down hills, staying in cottages and farm houses and listening to the speech of the people, hearing their stories and absorbing the beauty of the countryside and the well-kept homesteads."

The letter continues on a more personal note:

'He was charming, witty and not in the least condescending to a very junior Curate. Miss Ewart may have told him of my interest in philosophy, because he introduced the subject into our conversation at dinner and very graciously showed an interest in my response. He spoke of his life as a boy in Belfast and of some of the people he

remembered in St. Mark's, Dundela, where his Hamilton grandfather was Rector.

I remember in the course of this conversation that he spoke about novels and he averred that he hated short novels and on the whole would not bother to read them.'

This scholarly Archbishop of the Church of Ireland (one of many Church of Ireland leaders who have 'graduated' from Lewis' home Church of St. Mark's) sums up his tribute.

'Nearly forty-five years after this encounter with C.S. Lewis the occasion is indelibly impressed on my mind. I remember him as a charming, humorous, forthright Christian who rejoiced in the company, in the good food and wine on that evening; and who held County Down in great affection.'

I am very grateful to Miss Ewart and other members of the Ewart family for their precious hospitality and for the great privilege which they gave me of meeting C.S. Lewis for a whole evening and discovering him to be a charming, sanguine, even jovial Christian who was very gracious to the third Curate in St. Mark's, Dundela.

Dr. Caird ends with:

' I hope that these few reminiscences may be of some use to you for your centenary remembrance of a superb scholar, a confident and humble Christian.'

This delightfully observant letter, which I have quoted at length, gives a special insight into Lewis when at the height of his powers he shared his company with a young Church of Ireland Curate.

We are reminded, too, of the relaxation which came on the home ground of Strandtown where he was surrounded by fellow villagers and his kith and kin. Donald Caird also experienced at close quarters the warmth and love with which Lewis and his brother (and often his father, too) were surrounded within the prestigious Ewart family. They were related to the Ewarts and they were readily adopted following the tragically early death of their mother.

The connection was a lifelong one. As Lewis often reminded us he and Warnie blossomed socially and culturally within the Ewart household in which they shared full membership. Equally, Lewis added much to the charmed circle which he helped to create.

Archbishop Caird called his letter to me 'only a slight detail which may add a little to your collection relating to C.S. Lewis. A pebble for your cairn.'

Some 'pebble'! What we have is a remarkable example of the lasting impression which C.S.L. made on those who were privileged to meet and talk with him in person. It also brings to light human aspects of the man which are all too easily forgotten, since he was in many ways a very private person. So private indeed that as he once explained to Gundreda, he preserved the privacy of Glenmachan in his Autobiography by describing it as a place called Mountbracken. Since when, many tourists have searched Standtown in vain for that particular Big House!

CHAPTER TEN

Let the Children Speak

C.S. Lewis may have been a very private Irishman, but he was always at ease with children and they with him. Together they get the chemistry right: his age enabled <u>him</u> to link up with a receding past and <u>they</u> were young enough to catch glimpses of the future. It is a delicate balance in nature which is hard to achieve, but for explorations of a higher order it is a prerequisite; every now and again we adults are privileged to encounter the sudden experience. I was jolted into such awareness at a recent University seminar when it was reported that thousands of children 'still write letters to Lewis because they are not aware he's dead'. Suddenly it came to me: 'Could it be that we adults are getting it all wrong? Could it be that the children know that C.S. Lewis is really alive?' Spontaneously, the truth became common property - our Lewis seminar agreed with one accord.

This revelation was later underlined in a conversation with my grandson, Iain, when he and his playmate Chris shared their Lewisian insights with me. Approving of my project, they pointed me once again to The Lion, The Witch and The Wardrobe and as Lewis would have done for any good book, urged me to read it time and time again. My grandson was in no doubt:

'The book is excellent, you just can't wait to see what happens on the next page. You have to be strong-willed to stop reading it. Everything seems so imaginary, yet so real, and the idea of walking into a wardrobe and being in a whole new world is great.'

Children really do believe that there is something for all of us in that beyond-the-wardrobe world. I was being urged to 'join the club'.

So in the spirit of Lewis' young disciples (of all ages) for a final word I turn to the children of his own neighbourhood.

My first child's impression comes from a neighbour who telephoned me one day to share a C.S.L. story from way back in 1951 when she was a child of five.

Penelope was at home with her father, a civil servant, when he entertained three literary friends - Arthur Greeves, Lewis' great friend from boyhood days; Forrest Reid, the much undervalued local author always highly recommended by Lewis; and the great man himself, C.S. Lewis. It had all the makings of a convivial literary occasion. For the little girl in the midst of it all it provided a lifelong happy memory.

As Penelope puts it:

'It was a very happy get together and though I couldn't take it all in I was excited when my father told me that his friends were famous writers. He told me their names.

One of them went over to the bookshelf and took down one of my books The Lion, The Witch and The Wardrobe saying: "Penny you've got one of my books, can I have a

look at it? "I said "yes" and he said "come and sit on my
knee and we'll read it together for I wrote it."

'And so we did. I sat on his knee and he read me the
opening part and told me what it was all about. He was
so friendly and easy to follow. Only much later did I get to
know how famous Jack Lewis, as he called himself, really
was, but to this day I can still remember sitting happily
on his knee, with his arm around me and taking me through
the story.

When he was finished he said: "Would you like me to
autograph the flyleaf for you to remember me by?" I said
"yes" and here is what he said:

Dear Penelope,

Jack Lewis wrote all this. He didn't draw a picture,
though. That is why the giant who had a beard in the pic-
ture on page 91 is clean-shaven in the picture at p.157.
This is wrong. Giants hardly ever shave because they can't
get razor blades of the right size.

This (down below) is Jack Lewis's ort gr autograph -
anyway this is how I sign my name.

C.S. Lewis

What a lovely way to give an autograph. It tells us why C.S.
Lewis was such a genius in his dealings with children. He could
relax with them and he entered into the fun of things. Note how he
pretended to this young 5-year old that his spelling was even more
atrocious than it sometimes was!

Little wonder that Penelope remembers the occasion as if it were
yesterday. The truth is that the children of East Belfast (and world-

wide) feel close to Lewis and know that they can talk to him and he to them.

Now forty-seven years after Penelope's joyful experience I turn to my final offering from the descendants of those days. I speak with the children of East Belfast and from a school I know well. It is Mersey Street Primary School in the heart of the shipyard district. This was an area much frequented by C.S. Lewis with his grandfather Richard, himself a ship builder and in his day a well-known local personality. Their house, 'Ty-Isa' is still nearby.

A group of 10-year olds in this School, under the guidance of their teacher, Carla Stewart, have undertaken a study of C.S. Lewis' Narnia Tales as part of a special Centenary year project. I spoke to them recently and shared some of my memories and material with them. It was an easy 'seminar' to give; they were fascinated by Lewis and his work. Their enthusiasm was catching; I learnt once more what the man was all about. The day I was there the children were writing letters to C.S. Lewis .

Here are a few samples of what they wrote:

Mersey Street Primary School
78 Mersey Street, Belfast.
Principal. David Smith
June 1998.

Dear Mr. Lewis,

My name is Scott Baine. I am ten years and I live in East Belfast where you used to live. I have read your books The Chronicles of Narnia. *I would like to ask you if Cair Paravel is really Belfast Castle.*

Our teacher read us a bit from your brother's memoirs. He says that you used to stay in a lot when you were little because it rained and that you envied modern children because we get out and about more. I 'm glad that you and Warnie were kept in 'Little Lea' a lot because if not little children would not have your stories.

> *Yours sincerely,*
> *(sgd) Scott Baine.*

Dear Mr. Lewis ,

My name is Alana Gray and I'm ten years old. I live in East Belfast near where you used to live. I have read your books about Narnia. I think that they are remarkable. I know that your grand-dad worked in the shipyard. My Granda Billie works in the shipyard.

In two years l'm going to Ashfield Girls High School near your old house 'Little Lea'.

I think it was awful kind of you to write all those magical stories for little children. I have lived in East Belfast all my life and I haven't seen a lot of enchanting things like fauns, witches and giants. Children can read your stories and see all of these things in their minds. Thank you very much!

> *Yours sincerely,*
> *(sgd) Alana Gray*

Dear Mr. Lewis,

I am Sarah Cochrane and I am eleven years old. I go to Mersey Street Primary in east Belfast, around the corner from where you used to live.

*I have read **The Chronicles of Narnia.** I think they are brilliant. I think that the best one is **The Lion, The Witch and The Wardrobe**.*

I read in a book that you and your brother used to make up stories about a place called 'Boxen'. Is 'Boxen' another name for Narnia?

Next year I am going to Ashfield and I'll probably walk by and see if I can see the lamp post or any of the other things in your Chronicles. I know that your grandfather worked in the shipyard which is just around the corner from our school.

Do you remember when you were asked if you were going to write any more stories about Narnia and you replied: "I'm afraid that I've said all I have to say about Narnia, but why don't you try to write one yourself?"

Maybe I will try and write one myself!

Yours sincerely
(sgd) Sarah Cochrane.

Dear Mr. Lewis,

*My name is Angela and I am ten years old. I live in East Belfast where you used to live. I have read the adventurous, enchanting **Chronicles of Narnia** and my favourite is **The Lion, The Witch and The Wardrobe**.*

Our teacher read us a bit out of Warnie's memoirs. He describes the Castlereagh Hills as strange, distant and unattainable. Is this where you got the idea for the Narnia hills?

I believe that your grandfather worked in the shipyard. So did mine.

In two years I am going to Ashfield Girl's High, around the corner from 'Little Lea'. One day I will drop by your old house and maybe even see a little faun carrying an umbrella!

I think we are so lucky to have such enchanting stories full of fauns, fairies and talking animals. There isn't much magic in East Belfast but when children read your stories they come into a magical world.

Yours sincerely,
(sgd) Angela Jehan.

I also told the children about letters I had received from famous Irish people who enjoyed the Narnia Tales. One was from Maeve Binchy, who has done so much in Ireland to bring good reading to a mass audience. She sent this message:

FROM MAEVE BINCHY, DALKEY, CO. DUBLIN - 20 APRIL, 1998:

*'I have always specially admired C.S. Lewis's children's books - I think **The Lion The Witch and The Wardrobe** is one of the most enticing titles of all time! It is good to know that in this Centenary Year, his magical Narnia stories are appealing to a new generation of children.'*

Maeve Binchy's message matched the spirit of the occasion. These children know what life at the sharp end is all about. Yet excitement and simple faith is reflected in their responses. It is a tribute to the power and benevolent presence of Lewis and it is good that they should be under such an influence. In the words of Sam

McAughtry, gifted writer from Ulster and something of a folk hero in Lewis' Strandtown: 'It is a comforting thought for those of us born and raised in battle-scarred Belfast that this wise and gifted writer first saw the light of day in our city. I don't think he was complex: he had just the Northern Irish gift of common sense to a degree that made him distinctly uncommon, thank God.'

With children like these of Mersey Street, and with the plaudits for C.S. Lewis which are being offered from every part of the Province and Island which he loved, C.S. Lewis is assured of a home-coming worthy-of his greatness in this Centenary Year. The comprehensiveness of his appeal is being acknowledged precisely at the moment in our island-home when we need the spiritual strength which his life and witness represent.

MAIREAD MAGUIRE, PEACE PEOPLE, 28TH JULY 1998

I discussed this hope recently with Mairead Maguire, Nobel Peace Prize holder - she shared my optimism. She sent me this letter about our great literary son and his appeal for children:

Peace People - 28 July 1998

Dear David,

Thank you for inviting me to say a few words about C.S. Lewis on the Centenary (29.11.98) of his birth.
*I reread his beautiful children's fairytale **The Lion, The Witch and The Wardrobe**. In this little masterpiece for children of all ages, one feels again the great qualities possessed by this 'man of our time-C.S. Lewis'. He is spiritual, gentle, feels the beauty of the natural world*

keenly, understands human frailty and has a deep faith in his personal God. His message to us from this little book comes clearly through. It is not to be afraid to face the demons and the unknown within ourselves for there is someone already there who will help us - who knows a deeper magic that will defeat any monster we may create for ourselves. His confidence in the love and joy of his God comes shining through. He was a man of peace, a reconciler, a believer in the goodness of people.

C.S. Lewis admits to having a different agenda to that of writing to amuse children when he says "a children's story is the best art form for something you have to say."

I feel his message, so eloquently and powerfully conveyed, is extremely relevant to our situation in Northern Ireland. His writings challenge us to take into our hearts the message of peace and reconciliation.

Shalom, (sgd) Mairead.
Mairead Maguire

This message from Mairead Maguire identifies the universality of Lewis' appeal at the precise moment when we need it most in our troubled world. Our literary son is being accorded a Céad mile Fáilte. It is a well deserved 'Hundred Thousand Welcomes' marking the homecoming of a great Irishman.

C.S. Lewis belongs to Belfast and the County Down;
he belongs to every Province of Ireland;
he belongs to Oxford and the wider world;
and he belongs to the Ages.

A CLOUD OF WITNESSES
Letters on C.S Lewis from Christian Leaders

Introduced by Rt.Rev.Harold Miller
Bishop of Down and Dromore

This is a book about an East Belfastman, by an East Belfast man. Both C.S. Lewis and David Bleakley were born in Strandtown village, separated only by the width of a football ground. The first grew up in a middle-class wealthy home; the second as a Christian socialist. Both are men of whom Belfast can be justly proud. I remember the surprise when I discovered, in my twenties that the famous C.S. Lewis was from my own home town, and the sense of pleasure in seeing the record of his baptism in the registers of St. Mark's Dundela. He was a Belfast man whom some would even want to describe as a 'saint', because of the profound effect his writings have had on so many generations. But we don't expect saintliness to emerge from the ordinary streets of our own city! He certainly was not a plaster-cast saint, and indeed drifted away from formal churchgoing in his youth, tempted by the intellectual attractions of atheism, but in his coming back to Christ afresh as an adult, he became one of the greatest apologists for the faith that the twentieth century has known. C.S. Lewis is a great reminder to the church of this generation of the power of creative genius captivated by the Spirit of God.

Harold Down and Dromore
2 April, 1998.

•••

From the Most Reverend Dr. Robin Eames,
Archbishop of Armagh.

C.S. LEWIS

As a former rector of St. Marks' Dundela I came to appreciate something of the life and influence of C.S. Lewis. He was born in 1898 in that parish of East Belfast and baptised in St. Marks where his grandfather, Thomas Robert Hamilton had served as rector for over 20 years. The young Lewis would have played as a child in the rectory on the Holywood Road next door.

For C.S. Lewis the struggle to find a faith which would be practical, realistic and genuine finally reached its climax in 1931 when he embraced - Christianity. His words 'I believe in Christianity as I believe that the sun has risen, not only because I see it, but by it I see everything else' represented the end of a pilgrimage which was to be marked from then on by his writings for both adults and children.

C.S. Lewis will always be for me someone whose connection with Ireland has never received the recognition it deserved. He was one of our greatest sons to leave these shores. His writings continue to provoke the deepest spiritual thought and his personal expression of Christian faith remains an eloquent encouragement to many who seek the light in the midst of apathy, secularism and doubt. Perhaps his own pilgrimage could best be described as an honest seeking based on integrity of thought.

18 April, 1997.

•••

**From the Most Reverend Dr. Sean Brady,
Archbishop of Armagh**

C.S. LEWIS

I am happy to add to the report being compiled on C.S. Lewis and to mark the Centenary of his birth which affords a welcome opportunity for celebration on behalf of all religious traditions in Ireland and beyond. I am particularly glad to acknowledge the links which C.S. Lewis had within my own Archdiocese, and in Co. Louth especially, where he spent occasional holidays in Annagassan and became an admirer of the work of Mother Mary Martin and her Medical Missionaries of Mary, who frequently cared for his brother, Warren, at Our Lady of Lourdes Hospital in Drogheda. Indeed, in reflecting upon ten years of their work, whilst staying in Drogheda's old 'White Horse Hotel', Lewis displayed his unerring gift for robustly championing 'mere' Christianity when he wrote:

> *"No other belief leaves anyone free to do what is being done in the Lourdes Hospital every day: to fight against death. Because Our Lord is risen we know that on one level it is an enemy already disarmed: but because we know that the natural level also is God's creation we cannot cease to fight against the death which mars it, as against all those other blemishes upon it, against pain and poverty, barbarism and ignorance. Because we love something else more than this world we love even this world better than those who know no other."*

This life-affirming evaluation of Christian faith and action which permeated his personal life and diverse writings is a constant source of inspiration to all of us engaged upon the task of evangelisation. His generous and inclusive expression of Christianity, which lies within the finest tradition of Irish spirituality, has ensured that his life and work remain accessible to all who call themselves Christian and present a constant challenge to those who are engaged in the work of reconciliation in Ireland, whose religious intolerance caused him great pain. As he said himself in Mere Christianity:

> *"If I have not directly helped the cause of Christian reunion ,I have perhaps made it clear why we ought to be reunited."*

It is right that Christians should celebrate together the significance of the life and work of this great Christian, our fellow countryman, and to offer the hope that his reconciling words may bear additional fruit in the land of his birth in his Centenary Year.

Sean Brady
15 April, 1997.

•••

From The Most Rev. Patrick Walsh,
Bishop of Down and Connor

C.S. LEWIS - His Significance for Ireland today.

C.S. Lewis was profoundly human - after all his roots were in Belfast. He understood people and what motivates them; he recognised the tragic flaw in human nature; he also believed that men and women were capable of dealing creatively and gracefully with difficulties. Confrontation with pain in childhood forced him to be realistic and honest with himself. The untimely death of his mother before his teens, the strained relationship with his father, his unhappiness away from home at school taught him that maturity comes by facing suffering, not by avoiding it.

True to the Northern temperament he worked his way through such experiences, reflecting deeply on them and responding to the challenges of growing up. This is why he is an optimist in his writings, positive in his attitude to himself, to others, and to his world. In a city that has suffered much in the century since his birth Lewis signifies the survival instinct that has made us a tough and resilient people in the best sense of that term, a people that meets and emerges from adversity with wisdom and dignity.

He was always a conscientious thinker, even when an atheist. Committed to the search for truth he followed that path wherever it led. He brought to his search a vivid imagination and a profoundly analytical mind. He embodies the Ulsterman and woman's intellectual tenacity, rigorous determination of spirit, fidelity to what one sees to be right. In his writing he does more than communicate theories and philosophies. He establishes relationships: first between himself and the reader, then between the reader and God. Always reasonable, balanced and truthful, he invites his readers to travel with him on the pilgrimage of discovery which led him from atheism to faith.

His themes and style make him eminently appealing to young people in particular. He treats of subjects that young people find richly preoccupying - reason and faith; the purpose of existence; religion and science; culture and community; the nature of the human person; sin and redemption; language and meaning; objectivity and subjectivism; emotions and relationships; morality and conscience.

In his style he is personable, free, easy, clear, jocular, serious, conversational, idiomatic, alert to his listener's next question, generous in outlook, sympathetic, gregarious, firm.

These are characteristics of thinking people in their teens and twenties throughout our country today. Youth respond to the C.S. Lewis approach. Though he died on the day President Kennedy was assassinated, he is still modern, contemporary, relevant a hundred years after his birth. Though a child of his own time, his ideas are universal; and his expression of those ideas is so down-to-earth, so in tune with humanity and its problems, so assured in its sincerity that his writing is timeless. Ireland now has come to the secular cross-roads that Oxford faced in Lewis' time. The issues he deals with (of the secular Society of Britain in the thirties and forties) are now of immediate concern especially to Christians here whose faith is challenged by the climate of our times.

His own strong and intelligent faith as an Apologist is still challenging. It confronts those who believe but do not question their faith; it challenges those who have lapsed from faith by not thinking; it re-opens discussion among those who have rejected traditional values in the name of scientific truth, free thinking, or the permissive liberality of the modern world.

Patrick Walsh
2 June, 1997.

•••

**From the Rt. Rev. Dr. Samuel Hutchinson,
Moderator of the General Assembly.**

The Presbyterian Church in Ireland

C.S. LEWIS

The standing of C.S. Lewis in the world of Christian theology is beyond dispute, for he is generally recognised as one of the most acute religious thinkers of our era. On one occasion Time Magazine referred to him as "the most quoted exponent of Christianity after Jesus Christ and St. Paul."

He was an outstanding scholar, having gained a Triple First from Oxford in English and Classics (including Philosophy), but he also had the great gift of being able to communicate profound ideas in ordinary language. As he himself wrote, "Any fool can write learned language; the vernacular is the real test. If you can't turn your faith into it, then either you don't understand it or you don't believe it."

His success in this area may be judged from the fact that nearly 35 years after his death his books are still selling well. There can be few manses that do not have at least one of his works on a study shelf.

It gives me special pleasure to learn that he was born in Belfast and spent his early years there. In its golden age Ireland was known as the "island of saints and scholars". Whatever may have happened to that reputation in recent years, it can be said of C.S. Lewis that he deserves both titles. The books he left behind him will be a "monumentum aere perennius" -a memorial more lasting than brass.

11 March, 1998.

•••

From the Reverend Dr. Norman W. Taggart, President, Methodist Church in Ireland

C.S. LEWIS

In the second half of the twentieth century C.S. Lewis has become one of the best known and most widely read apologists for Christian orthodoxy. For example, I found that his books were known and valued in Sri Lanka, where I was working a few years ago. It is a tendency of our times to attempt to debunk such heroes, exposing the truth beneath the reputation. Lewis emerges largely unscathed from such attacks.

Lewis' honesty is one of the most compelling features of his writing. In his autobiographical books be makes no secret of his failures and his doubts, whether he is describing the intellectual and moral struggle which preceded his conversion or his grief following the death of his wife. His presentation of Christian doctrine and ethics is vigorous and uncompromising. He never waters down their challenge to our thinking and our lifestyle.

He was a natural teacher and communicator. Many of his books originated as lectures or broadcast talks. His writing is clear and straightforward, full of vivid images and illustrations. As a student and teacher of literature he understood that truth is often communicated most memorably and effectively in stories. His children's stories, science fiction and fantasy are not only a good read, but communicate the Christian values which informed his life and thinking. All his writing conveys a strong sense of the reality both of God and of evil. The range and variety is impressive and every reader will have his or her favourites, whether it be Mere Christianity or The Chronicles of Narnia, the Screwtape Letters or A Grief Observed.

Lewis became well known as a speaker and writer on Christian subjects at a time when those who held orthodox views about Christian doctrine and morality felt themselves to be increasingly under attack. They were strengthened by his fresh and lively defence of traditional Christianity while sceptics were encouraged to think again. Lewis is difficult to 'label', being greatly admired within both Roman Catholic and conservative evangelical traditions. As we mark the centenary of his birth in the land of his birth, Irish Christians of all denominations, living in an increasingly secular, materialistic and superstitious world, would do well to work together to celebrate and proclaim what unites us rather than arguing about what divides us.

20 March, 1998.

•••

From Pastor Joshua Thompson,
former General Secretary, Baptist Union of Ireland

It is always pleasing to know of a fellow-countryman who has gained world-wide recognition. C.S. Lewis became well known for his scholarship in academic circles: his gift for storytelling, however, made him well known and highly regarded by the general public.

I remember introducing our own children to The Lion, The Witch and The Wardrobe and the whole range of C.S. Lewis' children's stories and science fiction. They did not think of him as a clever allegorist, an outstanding Medieval scholar or an apologist for Christianity, but simply as a teller of entertaining stories, which they read avidly. We enjoyed reading Lewis ourselves and note his continued relevance to the present generation as we see our grandchildren beginning to read him for themselves.

His stories have a sound moral basis; he has used his scholarship and his imagination to make concepts of good and evil intelligible to ordinary people, and to articulate his personal struggle towards the belief in God which informed his life.

As a Pastor seeking answers to the human condition, I recall with gratitude the first time I read C.S. Lewis' wise comments on the imprecatory Psalms. His plea on prayer I have often made my own: "Take not, oh lord, our literal sense. Lord, in thy great, unbroken speech our limping metaphor translate."

Joshua Thompson
29 May, 1998.

•••

From Pastor Derick Bingham

Christian writing needs to get past the Watchful Dragons to ever penetrate the enemy's kingdom. Those dragons did not notice the man from Belfast, in his tweeds and cords, giving them the slip. They have been regretting it ever since. He has caused havoc far behind enemy lines to this very day. Even now, as the Scriptures say, "He being dead yet speaks".

Jesus, the Teacher above all teachers, taught from everyday things and people, particularly the masses, heard Him gladly. The enemy couldn't stand it, though, and had Him crucified. C.S. Lewis had his cross to bear in Academia for being a hugely popular writer, especially as he reached out to millions of children through his allegories with the good news of Jesus Christ.

As a County Down man I am hugely proud that C.S. Lewis revelled in its beauty and that its hills, lakes and shorelines provided him with inspiration for his writing. It is also wonderful to know that thousands of children all across Northern Ireland at Key Stage 2 have the unique and unprecedented resource of an Inter-Board Religious Education Project on the life of C.S. Lewis to study. It is a superbly thought out and fascinating piece of work.

C.S. Lewis' surrender to Jesus Christ as Lord and Saviour, despite all his doubts and fears and questions has proved to be one of the most inspiring lights in my own journey of faith. He is one of those members of the "cloud of witnesses" who have gone on ahead as mentioned in the letter to the Hebrews in the Bible, who helps those on their way to keep going. His definition of Heaven at the end of that journey as being "up from the garden to the Gardener, from the sword to the Smith, to the life-giving Life and the beauty that makes beautiful ... the term is over; the holidays have begun. The dream is ended; this is the morning", makes me want to long to see it.

As many of us flounder about in the dark wardrobe of sectarianism that plagues this land, and out of which I sometimes fear I shall never break, Lewis assures me that just out there I shall begin "Chapter 1 of the Great Story, which no-one on earth has read: which goes on for ever in which each chapter is better than the one before". I can't wait!

Derick Bingham
11 April, 1998.

•••

From Dr. Billy Graham, Evangelistic Association, USA

A SUMMING UP BY DR. BILLY GRAHAM THE GREAT
AMERICAN FRIEND OF C.S. LEWIS

We celebrate in the year 1998, the one hundredth birthday of one of this century's most valued and articulate Christians. A native of Belfast, C.S. Lewis was a truly remarkable figure - scholar, professor, renowned author of science fiction and fantasy, perceptive thinker and philosopher, and deeply committed Christian. It was my privilege to know this favourite son of Ireland.

I vividly remember my first encounter with C.S. Lewis, now some forty years ago. My friend, John Stott was anxious for me to meet Professor Lewis, when I visited Cambridge University during one of my many trips to Great Britain. I was nervous at the prospect of this meeting - after all what would this American evangelist have in common with this celebrated man of letters and education? He immediately put me at ease with his gentle and gracious manner. I came away touched by his relationship in both heart and mind with Jesus Christ.

In the personal story of his pilgrimage of faith, Surprised by Joy, Lewis recounts his journey from atheism through agnosticism to faith in the living Christ. This classic Christian work underscores his belief that once convinced of the truth of the Gospel through a personal relationship with Christ his unique talents and gifts would be used for the glory of God. Through his writing he consistently defended the historic tenets of the Christian faith, seeking often to reach those who had rejected the Gospel or who did not understand it. His considerable talents were waged against the tide of secular philosophies by clearly communicating the truth of the Gospel.

C.S. Lewis was also an ecumenical leader - a Christian whose reconciling spirit sought to bring people together. He was larger than any denominational label could describe or traditional stereotype could hold. His concern in declaring the historic core of Christian theology was to defend the faith in the face of ever increasing secular and humanistic philosophies. That was his significance - standing for the truths of the Gospel while reaching across the spectrum to all believers who share that truth.

I commend this historic celebration that will reach from Lewis' native land of Ireland to the whole world - a world of people who have benefited from this unassuming and humble spiritual giant. C.S. Lewis would probably have been a bit overwhelmed and embarrassed by this sort of attention, but he is undoubtedly one of the great Christian figures of this century. May this celebration of his life encourage all of us in the church to continue his work of confronting a sceptical and unbelieving generation with truth of the Gospel of our Lord and Saviour Jesus Christ. That was the mandate of C.S. Lewis and we who remain can do no less.

22 August, 1997.

•••

A Personal Note from David Bleakley

I am deeply grateful to all who have written to me and I welcome the opportunity to share their messages with a wider public. The letters in this Cloud of Witness offer comment on C.S. Lewis from Christian leaders representing much that is central to Irish life. The writers know their people and are well placed to appreciate the importance of Lewis for our time.

Down the years I have witnessed together with my correspondents - they as clergy and I as laity. I have enjoyed the Fellowship; it has been a privilege and pleasure to share in the pilgrimage. Our latest joint venture is an additional assurance.

The letters have been printed in full and as they were received. They speak for themselves and I have let them do so. However, it is good to see the splendid coming together which the occasion has afforded.

Lewis, I feel sure, would have liked this united witness from Ireland. What a book he could have written in response!

Yours sincerely,

David Bleakley
November 1998.

APPENDICES

C.S Lewis in St.Mark's, Dundela

Old Inn at Crawsfordsburn

Miscellaneous Letters

Family Documents

Big Houses - map

Useful Lewis Contacts

Acknowledgements

Chapter Themes

A Guide by Tony Wilson

C live Staples Lewis, the notable Christian writer, was baptised in the font at the west end of the church on January 29th 1899 by his grandfather, the Rev. Thomas Hamilton, Rector of St.Mark's.

We shall celebrate the centenary of his baptism in January 1999. If you wish to look for the objects associated with C.S Lewis in this church, follow the path shown by arrows in the plan and the words in italics in this guide.

The pilgrimage of life begins with Baptism at the font. When you stand here in the baptistery, remember that this man was called, almost against his will, to serve God by writing and speaking about 'mere Christianity', philosophical books and science fiction, in childrens' stories and on the radio. Many thousands have heard and are hearing his message, for his books still sell in great numbers all over the world.

Look toward the Communion table at the east end of the church. See how the architect, William Butterfield, has designed it so that the table, from which worshippers receive the bread and wine of Communion, is the most important object in the church standing higher (and therefore more important) than the pulpit from where the preacher preaches, or the lectern from which the Bible is read.

William Butterfield (1814-1900) was an Englishman who designed a large number of churches in England and aboard, according to the ideas of the Tractarian Movement. This was a religious revival which aimed to renew the faith of the Anglican Church by providing symbolic decoration in each church building to express ideas of worship. Butterfield used powerful, vigorous arches and pillars and walls in his buildings, decorated with multi-coloured stripes and patterns of stone and brickwork.

Follow the arrows which lead you along the nave between the pews to a point halfway up the church. Look to your right.

C.S. Lewis and his brother, Warren, known as 'Warnie', presented this window to the church in 1935 in memory of their father and mother. Three Saints are shown: two Gospel writers, St Mark and St Luke on either side of St James. We may wonder why St James, the son of Zebedee, is the central figure. Perhaps because the shrine at Compostela in Spain was a medieval place of pilgrimage - the pilgrim's bag and staff and the pilgrim's badge, the scallop shell shown in the window hint at this. But perhaps simply because Albert Lewis' second name was James. The Saint bolds a silver chalice, similar to one which Albert and his family presented to the church in 1908 in memory of their father, Richard Lewis, engineer and shipbuilder, who lived at Ty-Isa, near the Holywood Arches.

The Latin inscription below the window is translated:

To the greater glory of God and dedicated to the memory of Albert James Lewis, who died on the 25th September 1929, aged 67, and also of his wife, Flora Augusta Hamilton, who died on the 23rd August 1908, aged 47.

The two brothers, Warnie and Jack (as he had always been called, since the age of 4 years old) were very pleased with the window when they made a special journey to Belfast to see it completed. It was created by the Irish artist, Michael Healy (1873-1941), a member of the Tower of Glass, a well-known group of stained - glass window artists of the time.

Walk down the aisle (the narrow side passage) to see the memorial window to the Rev. Thomas Hamilton, first Rector of St. Marks (1826-1905). He was C.S Lewis' grandfather and baptized him. His daughter, Flora, Lewis' mother, died when the boy Jack was only 9 years old and this grievous loss stayed with the grown man all his life.

Now look at the lectern with its open Bible - the eagle is the symbol of St John the Gospel writer and represents the Word of God being carried on eagle's wings across the world. The Lectern was presented to the church by cousins of C.S. Lewis. The Lewis family sat in one of the front pews close to the pulpit, so the boy Jack would have been right under the eye of his grandfather, while he was preaching the sermon.

Stand and look up towards the Communion table. Notice how the tiles on the floor of the chancel are more highly decorated than the floor you are standing on. Then walk up between the choir stalls to the sanctuary. Do not go pass the railings. Again the tiles are even more highly decorative, symbolising the near approach to the Communion Table. Above it the letters IHS are perhaps a shortened form of the Greek name of Jesus.

The east window is a memorial to Isabella, Lady Ewart, the wife of Sir William, a wealthy linen magnate, who was one of the founders of St Mark's church. The nave, aisles and tower were built in 1878 and the chancel and transepts were added in 1891 at the expense of the Ewart family, as a memorial to Sir William. On the south wall of the sanctuary is the tablet which records his life and Christian service. His son, Sir William Quartus Ewart, is remembered in the window of the side chapel in the south transept.

His wife, Mary Warren Heard, was a cousin and dear friend of Flora Hamilton. So the Lewis boys were often invited to the Ewart's house, Glenmachan. C.S. Lewis in his autobiography, "Surprised by Joy" has much to say about the family. It was Cousin Mary, he records, who 'took upon herself the heroic work of civilising my brother and me'.

In this church and among these families young Jack Lewis grew up. After his mother's death, he was sent away to boarding school in England and his life was totally changed. Although as a young man he and his father grew apart, yet he never lost his fond memories of childhood in Strandstown.

The Old Inn at Crawfordsburn
- est. 1614

by David Bleakley - based on the Archives of the Inn

The Old Inn at Crawfordsburn stands on one of Ireland's most ancient highways leading from Holywood Priory to the Parent Abbey at Bangor, founded by St.Comgall as a University in 570 AD. Since then it has become a place of pilgrimage and worship.

Here much of the music of the early church was written, some of which is preserved in Milan where it was sent for safe-keeping during the Viking raids of the 10th century.

Part of a student's discipline in the ancient colleges of Bangor included the grinding of his own meal supply and for this purpose he was given a quern grindstone carved with the sign of the cross, one of which is to be seen in the Hall of the Inn.

The thatched portion of the building is the most ancient and was founded probably about the close of the reign of Queen Elizabeth I.

Records show this building to be standing in its present form in 1614. Substantial additions were made in the middle of the 18th century comprising of the kitchen quarters and several of the upstairs bedrooms. The East wing is modern, based on the Irish Georgian times. The buildings of the Inn fit well into the delightfully preserved village of contemporary Crawfordsburn, of which they are an integral part.

In the 17th and 18th centuries, Donaghadee was one of the principal cross channel ports between Ireland and Great Britain. The mail coach making connections with the sailing packet changed horses at the Old Inn at Crawfordsburn and so it came to be patronised by many notable persons. Famous writers were much in evidence: Swift, Tennyson, Thackeray, Dickens and Trollope knew of its charms.

The Inn was also used as a sanctuary for those employed in more physical pursuits. For example,a portion of William III's army under the Duke of Schomberg made use of the Old Inn when they passed through Crawfordsburn, on their way from Groomsport to join the main body of the forces at Belfast. The Inn was also used by smugglers down to the close of the 18th century and secret hiding places for contraband were discovered well into the 20th century. The famous Paul Jones was familiar with this part of the country and is thought to have patronised the Old Inn, though this a matter of some speculation. Dick Turpin during a period of hiding in Ireland, is said to have been a visitor here. There is also a persistent tradition that Peter The Great, Czar of Russia, called at Crawfordsburn during a visit to Ulster to study the latest development in the manufacture of damask, for which the Province is renowned. The tradition continues and many famous names in contemporary Ireland, and especially Co.Down, have used the Inn as a convenient meeting place for historic discussions. But for modern Lewisians the Old Inn is special. It is here that C.S Lewis and Joy found great happiness on their visit in 1958. And it was also here that Lewis and Greeves with other literary friends met on many social occasions.

During the C. S. Lewis Centenary Celebrations the Old Inn has been the meeting place for many national and international literary events.

D. B. November, 1998

Miscellaneous Letters
and Family Documents

From Professor Lionel Elvin my Principal when at Ruskin College, Oxford - remarking on C. S. Lewis.

Margaret and Lionel Elvin
Cambridge,
CB3 0EN.

Dear David,

When I said that you should follow up your chance meeting with C.S. Lewis, I had heard him lecture in Cambridge and had read the book that made his scholarly reputation. Its title was Prolegomena to Medieval Studies. This was before the Narnia books which Margaret read to our then young son. My other contact with him, was through Frank Quinn, who must have been a near contemporary of yours at Ruskin. I helped to get him into Magdalen and there Lewis took him under his wing and got him his first post as a lecturer at Haverford College in Pennsylavia. Frank was of a Catholic background but had no religion himself and said to Lewis that this would hardly commend him to a Quaker college. Lewis replied, very much to his credit, "You talk about English literature and if the   question of religion arises leave that to me".

I may have told you this. Frank Quinn, I am sorry to say, died a few months ago. I am sorry I cannot do more.

With every good wish,
LIONEL

28 February, 1996

•••

This 1955 letter from C.S Lewis to Gundreda Ewart explains why in "Surprised by Joy" he describes Glenmachan as Mountbracken. (We are indebted to Primrose Henderson - daughter of Gundreda, for preserving the letter in the Ewart archives.)

The Kilns,
Headington Quarry,
Oxford.
27/12/55

My dear Gundreda,

Thanks very much for your letter. I am relieved to find that the Mountbracken part was acceptable, for writing about old friends is a tricky business. I hope you thought my attempt at K's profile was successful and saw what I meant?. I hope she didn't get merely the general impression that I said that she was like a horse !

I wish now I'd put in something about both Graham and Palmer, "we shall not look upon their likes again." No, I didn't agree that the streamlined car is more useful than the large beautifully run house.

One's in the car at times:the house is affecting one all day and all night.

Warnie is in splendid health and form and has been for months; me too. You didn't say a word about Adrian, Primrose or Kelsie, so I hope that means they're all well. Give Warnie's and my love to them all, and to Janie and to yourself.

Yours affectionate cousin,

Jack

I'm sorry my writing is so horrid; the harder I try, the more illegible it seems to get!

The Kilns
Headington Quarry,
Oxford.

27 / 12 / 55

My dear Gurdus

Thanks very much for your letter. I am relieved to find that the Mountbracken part was acceptable, for writing about old friends is a tricky business. I hope you thought my attempt at K's profile was successful and saw what I meant? And I hope she didn't get merely the general im- -pression that I said she was like a horse! I wish now I'd put in some- -thing about both Graham and Palmer, "we shall not look upon their likes again.

No, I don't agree that the streamlined car is more useful than the large box

-ifully run house. One's in the car only at
times: the house is affecting one all day
and all night.

Warnie is in splendid health & form
and has been for months; me too.

You don't say a word about Adrian,
Primrose, or else, so I hope that means
they're all well. Give Warnie's & my
loves to them all, and to Janie, and
to yourself.

yours affectionate cousin

Jack.

I'm sorry my writing is so horrid; the
harder I try, the more illegible it
seems to get.

In October 1998 I sent this 'Lewis - man for the millennium' letter to the Sunday Times (London). It was published under the heading, 'Give Lewis dome room' - on Sunday 11 October, 1998.

8 October, 1998

Editor,
Letters,
Sunday Times.

Sir,

Your excellent Focus piece (4th Oct) on the significance of C. S. Lewis comes at a moment when we in Ireland are exploring 'Lewis territory' as never before.

In the process our people are learning much about Lewis' reconciling potential for our land and his capacity to encourage us on the peace pilgrimage.

But Irish Lewisians are equally aware that C. S. Lewis belongs also to a wider constituency - to Oxford, to Europe, to the world. In particular, we are deeply conscious of the ecumenical outreach of our great saint and scholar.

So would it be possible for London to offer spiritual 'space' to C. S. Lewis in that planned world gathering centre, the Millennium Dome? For instance, could we have a 'Wardrobe' area through which children of all ages might pass to savour the transforming magic which is Lewis?

Yours sincerely,

David Bleakley
Bangor, Co. Down.

MATRICULATED STUDENTS.

FACULTY OF ARTS.

Name (in full)? *Florence A. Hamilton*   Age, *23*

Place and Date of Birth? *18th May 1862. Queenstown*

If born in Ireland, in what Province? *Co. Cork.*

Father's Name, Occupation, and Place of Residence? *Rev. J. R. Hamilton Clergyman, Sydenham Park. Strandtown*

Religious Denomination? *Church of Ireland*

At what School were you educated? *Methodist Coll. Belfast*

Are you a Matriculated Student of the Royal University? *Yes*

If so, state the year in which you passed the Matriculation Examination? *1882*

Specify any other Examinations you have passed in the Royal University, and the dates of your passing them? *First Examination in Arts 1884, Second Examination in Arts 1885*

Are you a Matriculated Student of any other University? *No*

Have you attended any other College than this? *No*

Have you attended this College before? *Yes*

If so, state in what Session you last attended? *1884 – 5*

Year of your Course in this College? *Third year*

Do you take the Course recommended by the Council? *No*

Specify the Classes you propose to attend? *Honour and Second year Mathematics Honour and Second year Mathematics Physics Physics*

Do you propose to compete for a Scholarship, and if so, which?

Residence in Belfast? *Sydenham Park Strandtown*

Signed, *Florence A. Hamilton*

Dated *6. Nov.* 188 *5*

C840B

WARNING – This certificate is NOT evidence of the identity of the person presenting it.

The Births and Deaths Registration (Northern Ireland) Order 1976, Article 34

CERTIFIED COPY OF   AN ENTRY OF BIRTH

BIRTHS registered in the District of   Castlereagh   No. 3   Belfast

Bk 11

No (1)	Date and Place of Birth (2)	*Name (if any) (3)	Sex (4)	Name and Surname and Dwelling-place of Father (5)	Name and Surname and Maiden Surname of Mother (6)	Rank or Profession of Father (7)	Signature, Qualification, and Residence of Informant (8)	When Registered (9)	Signature of Registrar (10)	Baptismal Name if added after Registration of Birth and Date (11)
130	18 95 Twenty Ninth November Dundela Villa Strandtown	Warren Hamilton	M	Albert James Lewis Dundela Villa Strandtown	Florence Augusta Lewis †† formerly Hamilton	Solicitor	Mary Lane present at birth 1. Ballyqueen off Fifth Avenue Belfast	18 95 Fourth James December O'Brien Registrar.	

Certified to be a true copy of an entry in a register in the custody of the Registrar General and given under the SEAL of the General Register Office, Belfast.

this ....23rd....... day of ......August...... 19 96

The Registrar General shall cause any certified copy of an entry given in the General Register Office to be stamped with the seal of the Office, of which judicial notice shall be taken.

CAUTION:– Any person who (1) falsifies any of the particulars on this certificate, or (2) uses a falsified Certificate as true, knowing it to be false, or (3) passes as genuine any reproduction of this certificate, knowing that the reproduction is not the Certified Copy, is liable to prosecution.

G.R.O.
£6.00
43572

WARNING – This certificate is NOT evidence of the identity of the person presenting it.

The Births and Deaths Registration (Northern Ireland) Order 1976, Article 34

CERTIFIED COPY OF

AN ENTRY OF BIRTH

C8407

Bk 13

BIRTHS registered in the District of   Urban Nº 13   Belfast

No (1)	Date and Place of Birth (2)	Name (if any) (3)	Sex (4)	Name and Surname and Dwelling place of Father (5)	Name and Surname and Maiden Surname of Mother (6)	Rank or Profession of Father (7)	Signature, Qualification, and Residence of Informant (8)	When Registered (9)	Signature of Registrar (10)	Baptismal Name if added after Registration of Birth and Date (11)
353	18 98 November Twenty Ninth Abraham	Robert Stephen	9b	Albert James Ferris Stewartstown	Theresa Angela Ferris formerly Hamilton	Miller	T. A. Ferris Mother Stewartstown	January Ninth 18 99	J. Ferris Registrar	

Certified to be a true copy of an entry in a register in the custody of the Registrar General and given under the SEAL of the General Register Office, Belfast.

this .... 23rd .... day of .... August .... 19 96 ....

The Registrar General shall cause any certified copy of an entry given in the General Register Office to be stamped with the seal of the Office, of which judicial notice shall be taken.

CAUTION:– Any person who (1) falsifies any of the particulars on this certificate, or (2) uses a falsified Certificate as true, knowing it to be false, or (3) passes as genuine any reproduction of this certificate, knowing that the reproduction is not the Certified Copy, is liable to prosecution.

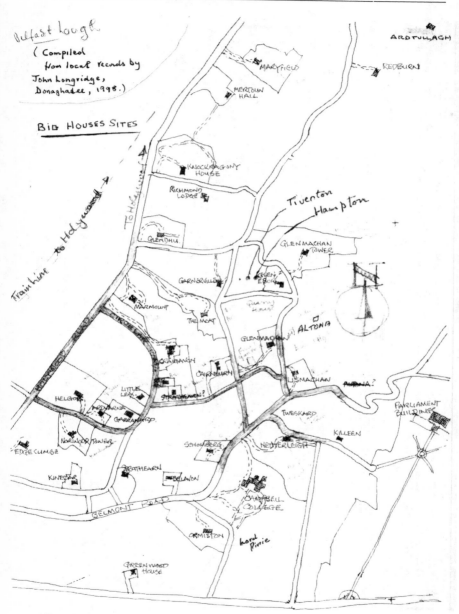

Big House Sites

Useful Lewis Contacts

C.S. LEWIS CENTENARY GROUP

11 Raglan Road, Bangor, Co.Down BT20 3TL,
Northern Ireland
Chairman: Mr. James O'Fee Tel:(01247) 473124
Hon Secretary: Mr Tony Fleck Tel/Fax: (01247)464401
Hon Treasurer: Mrs Joan Whiteside
Email:cslewis@dnet.co.uk
Web site: http://www.d-n-a.net/users/cslewis

THE LEWIS CENTENARY CELEBRATIONS IN ULSTER: NOTE BY JAMES O'FEE

In the summer of 1994 a Franciscan Friar returned from South Africa to his native Belfast. The Friar had become interested while abroad in the writings of C.S Lewis and had even written an article with the dateline "Belfast , South Africa". Home again, he wanted to find out more about the author in the city where both Lewis and he had been born.

Saddened by the lack of any memorial to the great Christian apologist in the city, the Friar wrote his own home-made leaflet "C.S Lewis and Belfast", describing some of the more important places in and around Belfast associated with the writer. He proposed celebrations in Ulster to mark the 1998 anniversary.

The Friar's name was Fr. Finbarr Flanagan, and his germ of an idea led to the first meeting in January 1995 of what became the C.S Lewis Centenary Group. Since then a group of us have met 4 or 5 times each year.

By 1997 we were well on the way. We decided to produce a brochure "The C.S Lewis Trail in Belfast and North Down", creating a Trail linking the Lewis sites. That summer we went on the Internet, created a web site, and led Guided Tours around the Lewis Trail. In the autumn we began to produce a monthly newsletter and published another brochure, the "C.S Lewis Centenary Programme of Event". We recruited a Lewis Research Fellow, Mr Ronald Bresland, based at Queen's University, Belfast, and created a Lewis Archive at the Public Record Office of Northern Ireland.

The autumn will see a Literary Festival in Co. Down and the unveiling at a public site in East Belfast of a Centenary Sculpture of the writer, and the performance of a memorial Concert in the City's prestigious Waterfront Centre.

To a large extent, our activities have been aimed at stimulating other people to take action. Projects of this type have included:

- a series of One-man shows given by Rev. Trevor Gillian, Rector of Aghalurcher Parish, Co. Fermanagh. The shows are set in Lewis' home in Oxford, "The Kilns".
- the Royal Mail C.S. Lewis Stamp
- the Belfast Lewis Conference
- the Lewis Statue

- Lewis displays and exhibitions at Belfast, Dublin and Cork libraries and at the Ulster Folk Museum
- Rt.Hon. David Bleakley's Centenary Biography "C.S Lewis - at Home in Ireland" - foreword by Walter Hooper, Strandtown Press , 8 BT19 1RD, Bangor, Co.Down, N.Ireland."

The ever helpful James O'Fee concludes:

"Whether we have been successful in increasing interest, locally and abroad, in Lewis, his writings and his Irish links is for others to judge. We have certainly tried."

Yes, indeed the Centenary Group has tried - and has been an outstanding success.

Membership at September 1998

Chairman: Mr. James O'Fee
Hon. Secretary: Mr. Tony Fleck
Hon. Treasurer: Mrs. Joan Whiteside
Cllr. Dr. Ian Adamson M.B., D.C.H., M.F.C.H
Rt.Hon David Bleakley, C.B.E
Mr. Aiden Flanagan
Fr. Finbarr Flanagan ofm
Mr. Peter Froggatt
Dr. John Gillespie
Rev. R.Trevor Gillian
Mr. Kenneth Irvine
Mr. Terry James
Rev. Jack Lamb
Miss Rhonda Paisley
Mr. Christopher Parker
Mr. Ian Sinclair
Mr. John Whiteside

Mr. Ross Wilson
Mr. Tony Wilson
Former Members
Mr. Jonathan Bardon
Mr. Michael Hutchison
Mrs. Hilary Trueick
Mrs. Sarah Jamison

USEFUL LEWIS SOURCES

1. East Belfast Historical Society: Chairman, J.Thompson Steele, 107 The Mount, East Belfast.
2. Jim Patton, Old Holywood Road, Belfast 4 and Noel Nesbitt, Belmont Road, Belfast 4 (local historians)
3. Keith Haines, Campbell College, Belfast 4
4. John Longridge, Donaghadee: "Big Houses"
5. Mary Rogers, Oxford (formerly Strandtown)
6. The Linen Hall Library, Belfast 1 (founded 1788)
7. Public Record Office of Northern Ireland, Malone Avenue, Belfast
8. Central Public Library, Royal Avenue, Belfast
9. The New University of Ulster, Coleraine, Co. Antrim.
10. Queen's University, Belfast

INTERNET CONTACTS

C.S. Lewis Centenary Group - http://dnausers.d-n-a.net/cslewis/home.html
C.S. Lewis Mega-Links Page - http://ic.net/~eramus/RAZ26.htm
St.Mark's Church, Dundela, Belfast - http://www.iol.ie/~coiace/lewis.html
The Author's Lewis web site - http://www.cix.co.uk/~cosine/cslewis/index.htm - email - davidbleakley@hotmail.com

Acknowledgements

This book has been a shared effort by hundreds of people who have joined in an Irish Quest for C.S. Lewis - pilgrims in a common cause, we have talked and reasoned together. I thank all who have helped. To those who have contacted me directly I have indicated gratitude in the text - Primrose and Bill Henderson have been particularly generous in their sharing of family memories. For many others, my 'Thank you' is composite. But it is not less meaningful; I trust that no-one will feel left out.

For writers on a long Journey it is always good to have the company of a small band of 'personal people', ever willing to give help with time and talents. Family folk, like Peter and Christine who have guided me through the mysteries of new technology - a world far removed from Lewis' homely pen and inkpot. I have survived the transition - but only just! I owe them much.

And other local special people who have been part of the out-come: Florence Pyper, always on hand to type-down what I have to say; Beatrice Stewart, patient and dedicated research assistant, who has finecombed the evidence indicated by me, while at the same time using her considerable Lewisian instincts to unearth new sources; and Ruby Purdy, another of my sisters-in-Lewis who has shared with me a unique memory bank, rich in the social history of Strandtown and its hinterland.

Our collective effort has been expressed in a new Irish Imprint, Strandtown Press, specifically created for the Centenary occasion. Fortunately we have had as our Master Printer Joe Costley, whose commitment and expertise has broken the daunting bondage of publishing 'deadlines'. And most of all, a home base for the 'Lewis in Ireland Quest' has been provided by Winnie, my wife of a life-time. Over many years she has had to contend with 'matters C.S.L.' - as she has been known to put it when yet another Editorial problem appeared: 'It's that man Lewis again, demanding attention!'

Thank you. Winnie, for putting up with the pair of us. We've been a 'right handful' at times.

All Good Company on the journey: C. S. Lewis would have been happy in the company and we with him.

David Bleakley
November, 1998

Chapter Themes

1. Prologue: origins of Biography

2. Irish Homecoming: neglect of Lewis as an Irishman, Seamus Heaney message, Ross Wilson statue, James Galway, President Mary McAleese.

3. Oxford and Cambridge: Lewis as teacher and friend, Mary Rogers, Mollie Reidy, Nansie Blackie, Simon Barrington-Ward.

4. Oxford Encounter: introductions, Lionel Elvin on Lewis, topics for conversation, family matters, Lewis and politics.

5. Cowley Fathers: SSJE, monastic life, Lewis and Confessor, note on Father Adams.

6. Lewis Genesis: formative influences at home, Anglo-Irish traditions, pattern of education, influence of World War I.

7. Home and Co. Down: Strandtown history, life at Little Lea, Big Houses, Ewart family link, Albert Lewis.

8. Places and People of Strandtown: domestic and social contacts, St. Mark's Church, Belmont Presbyterian, family contacts.

9. Voices from Strandtown: local personalities.

10. Let the Children Speak: a school in East Belfast.

    Finally - A Cloud of Witnesses ... selection of letters from Christians.